The Conscience
of the Campus

The Conscience of the Campus

Case Studies in Moral Reasoning Among Today's College Students

JOSEPH DILLON DAVEY
AND LINDA DUBOIS DAVEY

Westport, Connecticut
London

4/2002

Library of Congress Cataloging-in-Publication Data

Davey, Joseph Dillon.
    The conscience of the campus : case studies in moral reasoning among today's
college students / Joseph Dillon Davey and Linda DuBois Davey.
      p. cm.
    Includes bibliographical references and index.
    ISBN 0–275–97208–9 (alk. paper)—ISBN 0–275–97211–9 (pbk. : alk. paper)
    1. College students—United States—Conduct of life—Case studies.
2. Education, Higher—Moral and ethical aspects—United States—Case
studies. 3. Ethics—United States—Case studies. 4. Moral education—
United States—Case studies. 5. United States—Moral conditions—Case
studies. I. Davey, Linda DuBois, 1943– II. Title.
LA229.D35 2001
378.1′98—dc21   00–064954

British Library Cataloguing in Publication Data is available.

Library of Congress Catalog Card Number: 00–064954
ISBN: 0–275–97208–9
ISBN: 0–275–97211–9 (pbk.)

First published in 2001

Praeger Publishers, 88 Post Road West, Westport, CT 06881
An imprint of Greenwood Publishing Group, Inc.
www.praeger.com

Printed in the United States of America

The paper used in this book complies with the
Permanent Paper Standard issued by the National
Information Standards Organization (Z39.48–1984).

10 9 8 7 6 5 4 3 2 1

To our parents: Ellen Hand DuBois, Mary Dillon Davey, and Joseph Aloysius Davey, through whom we were first introduced to questions of morality and conscience; and to our newest grandchildren: Nell, Rose, Garrett, Dillon, Fiona, Joseph, and Timothy, with whom we hope to continue the conversation.

Contents

Preface

This book is about conscience development in the college community. Specifically, it uses examples from actual classroom experiences to describe how college students think about the moral issues of the day as well as how to use these examples to promote critical thinking skills.

We believe that for a society to thrive, especially one as diverse in culture and religious beliefs as ours, we need to encourage the higher-level thinking processes that develop, like a muscle, through the exercise of the brain. We are not interested here in describing the transfer of some set of rules or principles that others may set up for groups to adhere to and that can be responded to with some agreed-upon, previously dictated behaviors. These rules and principles offer excellent guidance for many, but we are concentrating on another aspect of the process of learning to do what is prudent. We seek to encourage the exchange of ideas and the difficult reflective analysis that comes with learning to reason things through to a just solution.

Recent research has shown that there is much previously unknown restructuring of the brain during adolescence. At this time, "The regions of the brain responsible for judgment, insight and planning are still immature" says psychologist Deborah Yurgelun-Todd (*Newsweek*, May 8, 2000). The restructuring of these areas during the teens and early twenties depends on how they're used during the "pruning" period. In terms of education, it is our belief that the development of conscience, independent of but not necessarily in conflict with any particular religious orientation, is as important to the outcomes for education as any other curriculum area. To leave the development of conscience to religious or professional groups alone denies some of our youth, at the very least, the ability to learn to think in a way that may be essential to their future—and ours.

Some time ago, a professor from a prestigious nonsectarian university spoke to a group of educators about the lack of ethical behavior recently noted in the graduate students of the business school. When a reading was assigned as "on reserve" in the library, she related, a *guard* had to be posted to keep students from stealing the article. If the first student to get to it could deny the others the opportunity to read the assignment, that student would have a competitive edge on grades. The speaker wondered aloud what such behavior would mean for the country when these very talented young people took the positions of business leadership for which they were being prepared. Her words seem haunting when we consider that the Savings and Loan debacle shook the nation a few years later.

The 21st century, which will belong to the students in school today, seems poised to deliver sweeping changes in the way we live and work. Information, for example, will be called up, not as much from memory banks as from computer banks. On all fronts, technology is moving with fierce swiftness to alter the boundaries of our thinking. Swept up in the pressures of the moment and its demands on us to grow and adjust, we may miss some important messages about what is needed now to prepare for this future.

The tomorrows of the 21st century, for example, will not be just bright additions to the status quo, something that can be displayed at a world's fair exposition. They will be qualitatively different from everything we know. Standing at the beginning of a new millennium, we can only glimpse the possibilities and changes the coming years will bring, but it is already apparent that technology is introducing us to worlds we may not be ready for. If we know nothing else, we should realize that the skills needed to govern our decision making in this brave new world of tomorrow will rely less on the accumulation of knowledge than on being able to both access and evaluate that knowledge as needed.

Not a day seems to pass without someone finding another moral crisis in our midst. Each new revelation brings us face to face with a reality more frightening than the one before it. We seek reasons and solutions in all quarters, but when all is said and done, the greatest moral crisis of our day may actually be the failure of schools and other institutions to adequately prepare the populace for conscientious thinking.

The development of thinking skills takes time and energy. It takes one-on-one interaction and an emphasis not merely on memory but on the development of higher-order thinking skills. Such divergent thinking is teased out in the interplay of shared ideas but this takes more time than the "sage-on-the-stage" approach frequently observed.

Several cognitive theorists have offered insight into this process. Jean Piaget pointed out that it is through arguments and the collision of ideas, especially with peers, that the reasoning processes grow and are transformed. Lev Vygotsky regarded dialogue as the essential element in cognitive development and believed that when skills for dialogue are modeled for, and practiced with, children, they can internalize aspects of the process and use these strategies, on their own, in future discussions. It may be time to recognize that even young adults can use such scaffolding help as they learn to dialogue reasonably.

Perhaps the thinking exercises in this book apply to no one outside of students of law and government more than teachers. Teachers at all levels of the educational process have a responsibility to pass on to future voters a thoughtful understanding of the government in which they function—and to do so in an objective yet knowledgeable way. Even more important, it is teachers who are charged with the task of preparing students for the future, and that future—more than ever before—involves the need to think, solve problems, and critically analyze the moral and ethical problems of the day.

The study of legal precedent provides a good avenue to stimulate such thinking because it is the very *stuff* of everyday conversation. The issues discussed in this book are the same ones splashed across the headlines as we head out to work and encountered repeatedly as sound bites on the airwaves. Unraveling legal precedent as a method of exploring our own sense of fairness and justice is one way that teachers and professors in all areas of study can connect to common understandings and interests.

In the cases that follow, there is no right and wrong. Occasionally, court decisions offer models of the reasoning process involved in arriving at a just decision but, for the reader, prudence only demands that we explore the issues and raise the level of dialogue to a point where it provokes critical thinking. Each teacher who chooses to utilize these scenarios for discussion should lead the group as a "more capable peer"—a so-called "guide by the side"—so that dialogue skills are challenged and expanded. By exploring these cases, students should be better able to explain, define, and defend a moral or ethical decision. Where they choose to take the discussions depends on the group and the teacher—and the subject at hand. Whatever the parameters, all our futures will be in better hands if more attention is paid to such areas of development. As John Dewey says:

> Not only is social life identical with communication, but all communication (and hence all social life) is educative. To be a recipient of a communication is to have an enlarged and changed experience. One shares in what another has thought and felt and in so far, meagerly or amply, has his own attitude modified. Nor is the one who communicates unaffected.[1]

NOTE

1. J. Dewey, *Democracy and education* (New York: The Free Press, 1916), 5.

Acknowledgments

We wish to thank all the students whose reasoning about "just" solutions forms the basis for this book. Because of their willingness to share in the difficult work of debating ideas, we have not only had the opportunity to enlarge and enrich our own understandings of issues that involve ethics and morality, but have been pushed to further reflect these understandings in our teaching.

We are grateful to our friends and colleagues at Hofstra University and Rowan University, whose intellectual and moral support has been invaluable to our own reasoning and whose professional ideals continue to enhance our joy in teaching. With appreciation, we also thank our mentors at Teachers College and CUNY Graduate Center who give so much of themselves in their efforts to stretch and refine thinking.

With love and admiration, we thank our children and their spouses. Their hopes for the future push us in our dream for the truly just society.

Introduction

Political leaders everywhere are talking about the importance of *moral education* in the public schools. They have finally begun to understand the difference between *religious education*, which is not allowed under the Constitution, and teaching moral and ethical principles to today's students. For far too long, public educators have avoided examining the moral values of their students. This has been attributable to either the mistaken belief that teaching morality was violating the wall of separation between church and state, or in the equally mistaken belief of the deconstructionists that there is no such thing as "right and wrong." This book encourages a change in that policy.

Many professors today like to quote Aristotle's observation that philosophy begins with leisure. In other words, it is only when people are free from the struggle to survive that they can contemplate the meaning of life. It is true that many students need to work to support themselves and their education. Nonetheless, contrary to their popular image, today's college students actually are interested in more than just finding a good job with financial security. When presented with the right moral dilemmas, they are genuinely interested in exploring the fine moral distinctions made by their peers, their professors and those very wise jurists who have contributed to that body of precedent known as the *common law*.

Many of today's students believe that they are not in control of their lives. They feel victimized by an enormous amount of social disruption, yet they are expected to be extremely autonomous. They look at a society where the family is under siege and where trying to find the "mainstream" amounts to chasing a moving target. They wish to explore their personal value systems because they want to forge a more reliable set of connections to the culture than those that they presently have. Virtually all these students feel less connected to their families, neighborhoods, churches, and workplaces than their parents and grandparents felt at their age; as a result, they are often lonely and disoriented. Many long for deeper and more permanent relationships and have a genuine interest in examining their own moral beliefs about such relationships.

A 1999 Gallup poll among the general public reflected a widespread interest in the morals of the nation. Almost 50 percent of respondents indicated that they believed the nation was in the midst of a "moral crisis" and another 41 percent said that morals was a "major problem."[1] College students do not differ markedly from the nine out of ten Americans who indicated their concern about morality to Gallup.

We have never needed their interest in moral distinctions more than we do now. As the new millennium begins, there are many highly nuanced social, legal, and political problems that will demand a higher level of moral awareness than the problems presented in less complex times. How should the law be fine-tuned so as to resolve the overwhelming problems facing contemporary families? What are the proper limits on government when it seeks to interfere with parents' control of their children? Or restrict a religious practice? Or regulate sexual behavior? Or the problems of race, poverty, drugs, violence, sexual excess or dysfunction? What kind of laws should govern the society in which today's students will raise and teach tomorrow's citizens?

College professors frequently complain about their inability to provoke their students into debates about value-laden issues. One approach to this problem is to come up with provocative scenarios presenting moral quandaries that touch the realities of student's lives as a way to encourage animated debates involving their values. This book presents twenty-five such scenarios (a third of which are U.S. Supreme Court cases) that have been presented to students in college classrooms over the last two decades and have been consistently successful at starting animated discussions about moral values. These debates deal with how the law can be used to translate society's most fundamental moral values into rules designed to achieve justice. How does understanding the logic of the law help us follow the pursuit of justice in a democracy? How should the law function as the conscience of the community?

This book offers two benefits to readers. First, it offers insights into the moral, legal, and political values of today's college students, a generation that is widely presumed to have little use for such values. Second, it gives professors a collection of compelling examples that have consistently touched off enthusiastic discussions in college classrooms.

The underlying question in these scenarios is always the same: Given the complex social problems in 21st-century America, how should we distinguish right from wrong in shaping the law? These scenarios encompass the changing consensus on issues such as gender roles, race relations, religious freedom, sexual behavior, family, marriage, violence, drugs, prison, poverty, and inequality. What is the appropriate social policy in these areas for a society that considers itself "just?"

It is widely believed that today's college students are too pragmatic to be interested in debating moral issues. These students are thought to be unusually fearful about their future, especially when it comes to earning a living. The employer loyalty and job stability that their grandparents experienced in the fifties and sixties disappeared for their parents' generation in the eighties and nineties. These students have seen their parents struggle through being downsized or relocated or treated like little more than a commodity by their employers, and they worry about their own careers. This fear, it is assumed, has caused them to become more self-absorbed and practical about their studies and less interested in the analysis of abstract values. This assumption has been grossly exaggerated.

First of all, the Gallup polls indicate that this generation actually places less importance on financial success than earlier generations. Finding the right mate and having time to raise a family rank higher in their values than in the polls done on their parents' generation. Perhaps they come to this value as a result of the upheaval they witnessed as children when widespread divorce was the norm among their parents' generation. Nonetheless, they do seem to be less materialistic than their parents' generation.

At the same time, even if they are not overly concerned about achieving financial success, they really are fearful about financial security. Will there be jobs for them? Will these jobs be fleeting and constantly threatened by foreign competition? Personal economic stability—as opposed to the acquisition of great wealth—is their first order of business. How they will earn a living is a constant concern for most of them.

But that does not mean that they are any less interested in examining their own values and making moral judgments about the world around them. However, opportunities for thoughtful exploration of ethical issues are not always readily available to today's youth. For America to continue to pursue its elusive goals of liberty and justice for all, each generation must be introduced to and practice procedures for mental debate, both intrapersonal and interpersonal, through which such abstractions as justice, morality, and ethical behavior will take meaningful shape.

In his influential *Theories of Justice*, Harvard's John Rawls argued that of all the virtues, justice is pre-eminent. But the meaning of the word *justice* depends on the moral values held by the individual offering the definition. The search for the meaning of justice is reflected in the literature of twenty-five centuries. In Plato's *Republic*, Socrates wrestled with definitions of justice without ever reaching a conclusion, and it is likely that this search will never end. But the pace of modern life has left little time for such lofty contemplation. Once students leave academia for the real world, they are often preoccupied with more immediate concerns. Unfortunately, for most professors it appears that there is less and less time for such contemplation even in college classrooms.

VALUE-FREE INSTRUCTION

All too many college professors have abandoned the hope of provoking philosophical discussion involving personal moral values in their classes. The unfortunate result is that while earlier generations could use their college years to heighten their moral awareness by discussing philosophical dilemmas, this generation of students is offered a "value-free" curriculum by professors who are reluctant to talk about right and wrong. As moral judgments are purged from class discussions, course content in classes in the social sciences and the humanities grows increasingly sterile.

It is difficult to find college professors today who do not believe that the students they encounter are more hesitant than ever to get involved in discussions of value-laden issues. They argue that unlike the students of the sixties, today's students require enormous coaxing before they will share moral and political views with others. More important, many of these professors believe that all moral quandaries are relative to the time, the place, and the culture in which they arise and it is therefore meaningless to engage in moral debate at all. Accordingly, today's professors frequently choose to avoid these discussions altogether.

There are probably many reasons for the initial reluctance on the part of today's students to discuss moral values. Increasingly, they have been raised in a society that seeks to be nonjudgmental when it comes to the ideas of others. Moreover, to some extent today's students are turned off by the media emphasis on character failure and the moral weakness of political leaders, religious leaders, and others in the public eye. Political campaigns consistently stress the most negative aspects of an opponent's character and the public in general has developed a thinly veiled contempt for politicians. To some extent, college students reflect these attitudes.

Moreover, the electronic media has played a major role in stimulating the cynicism that the public feels about moral heroes. There is an inherent need in the media for ever-more-sensational stories to stimulate their audience. The greater the moral failure discovered by the press in the life of a reputable member of the community, the higher the Nielson ratings will be when the story is aired again and again. Twenty-four-hour-a-day cable coverage of government officials has touched off a sequence of events that culminates in increased cynicism among today's students and a certain confusion about moral standards. They are a generation with very few landmarks on their moral horizon. And the truth is, they need such landmarks.

The Greek word *idiotes* means someone who is private or isolated or uninterested in public problems. Our word *idiot* is derived from *idiotes* and, while it has taken on a different meaning today, it is probably the best word to describe an individual who has no interest in the burning political issues of the day. When students hear this, they always seem a little bit uneasy, as if it might be followed by some questions about current controversies in the fields of law, politics, and social justice—issues about which they might be uninformed. However, once this initial reluctance is dealt with and they are presented with fact patterns that call for and expect moral reasoning, the floodgates open.

In short, we have found college students to be almost universal in their desire for more discussions of the moral, legal, and political dilemmas that confront them and their future. The following scenarios are the ones we found most provocative. The underlying question presented is always the same: "What is justice in this situation?"

TEACHING VALUES TO UNDERGRADUATES

Students today seem to sense that we are in a period of social transition that will require major changes in the law as the legal system attempts to catch up with social changes. What should the law say about some of these changes? Should frozen embryos be awarded as part of a property settlement in a divorce? Should grandparents have visitation rights over a widowed son-in-law's objection? Do mandatory retirement ages make sense now that sixty-five does not mean what sixty-five used to mean?

Transformative moments in the legal tradition of a nation are always painful. Old paradigms crumble and take with them the binding mythology that can offer the comfort of stability. It may well be that there has never been a time when college students were more eager to discuss fundamental questions about right and wrong; to examine their own moral values and to find some conclusions about what they personally believe is morally correct. The ideal role that law can play in a free society is to function as the conscience of society. Law in its purest form is supposed to be the tool with which the political system sets standards and values for the community, based on the public's moral consensus. Is a "partial birth abortion" a moral act? What should the law be concerning physician-assisted suicide? Should gay couples be allowed to marry? Or adopt children?

The goal in every class in the social sciences should be to encourage students to understand how political leaders help bring about social justice by using the law as a tool. The concept of *social justice* is a controversial one, and reasonable people may disagree on its meaning. In a democracy, everyone has an obligation to examine his or her own fundamental values concerning issues of social justice. Therefore, students should be challenged to apply their sense of right and wrong—their morals and ethics and philosophical or religious views—to take a position on the burning issues of the day.

But what should the law be concerning issues about which there is no public consensus? Abortion, the death penalty, pornography, homosexuality, or gun control—what should the law be on these issues? Homosexual behavior is currently a crime in half of the fifty states. In the other states, it is legal. The death penalty is legal in thirty-seven states and not allowed in the other thirteen. Abortion laws vary widely throughout the nation, as do drug and gun laws. Prostitution and gambling are legal in Nevada, while alcohol is banned in many counties all over the nation.

Even more complex moral issues are currently being debated about the whole concept of life and death. The nature of life was something that earlier generations thought was pretty clear. But today questions of when life begins, and how and when it ends, can start a heated argument. Students may have already formed an opinion about these issues. It is more useful for students to debate the morality of legal issues about which they have not already locked in an opinion. More subtle problems tend to provoke more interesting discussion. Topics like physician-assisted suicide, or government standards for child abuse, or rejection of medical help for children on religious grounds never fail to bring out strongly felt opinions in today's college students. Nonetheless, after listening to the views of their fellow students, they sometimes find themselves abandoning their views and switching sides. What better use of time in a college classroom?

NOTE

1. G. Gallup, *The Gallup Poll Monthly* (Princeton, NJ: The Gallup Poll, February 8, 1999).

SUGGESTED READINGS

Berkowitz, M.W. & Gibbs, J.C. (1985). The process of moral conflict resolution and moral development. In M.W. Berkowitz (Ed.), *Peer conflict and psychological growth*. San Francisco: Jossey-Bass.

Berman, E. (1999). Morality and the goals of development. In M. Woodhead, D. Faulkner & K. Littleton. (Eds.), *Making sense of moral development* (pp. 170–180). New York: Routledge.

Gilligan, C. (1995). Moral orientation and moral development. In V. Held (Ed.), *Justice and care: Essential readings in feminist ethics* (pp. 31–64). Boulder, CO: Westview Press.

Kohlberg, L. (1970). Education for justice. In J.M. Gustafson (Ed.), *Moral education: Five lectures* (pp. 57–65). Cambridge, MA: Harvard University Press.

Lipman, M. (1988). Critical thinking—What can it be? *Educational Leadership, 46*(1), 38–43.

Noddings, N. (1994). Conversations on moral education. *Journal of Moral Education, 23*, 107–118.

Chapter 1

Law as a Guide to Justice

Jefferson said that for the law to be "just" it should be a codification of public opinion. How well does the public agree on what "justice" means?

The image that college students have of the law in the United States today is not what it should be. Many students see the legal system as a process by which people strive to avoid justice through sophistry and loopholes rather than achieving justice through rational deliberation. A large proportion of today's students believe most lawyers are morally and ethically bankrupt, located, on a moral scale, somewhere below used car salesmen and slightly above drug dealers. Lawyers do not get a great deal of respect in college classrooms these days.

A majority of college students also believe that there are just too many lawyers and far too many laws, usually referred to as "technicalities." The argument they make is usually framed as follows: If the function of law is to guide us in our search for justice, and everyone has an innate feeling for what is fair and unfair, then why do we need Harvard-trained legal scholars to help us do the just thing? We know what is just and unjust. We are born with a sense of fairness—we call it a conscience—and we can determine what is the just thing to do in any given case. So why are there 700,000 lawyers gumming up the works?

One student making this argument gave this simple example: "Ask any five-year-old what is the right thing to do when Noelle steals a cookie, Chris gets falsely blamed for the theft by Mommy, and Chris gets sent to bed. What is it that the five-year-old will say about that situation? 'That's not fair,' she will tell you. Even little Noelle, the beneficiary of the injustice, will know at some level that this is 'not fair.' " So why do we need law as a guide to justice? The standard response, of course, is that adult life is more complex than stealing cookies and legal problems develop where "the just thing to do" is not obvious to the average person. As the problems become more complex we find that reasonable people disagree as to what *justice* demands. We need the guidance of legal precedent to find the just thing to do.

As a way of demonstrating this point, it is helpful to consider examples of legal cases in which "the just thing to do" is not always clear. In fact, it can be confidently predicted that students will disagree with one another in almost equal numbers about what justice demands in this situation. Consider Barbara Fisher and her son:

Suing Mom

Barbara Fisher called her son, Carl, to see if he could get her car started. Her son was a car mechanic and when he examined the car he told his mom that it was going to need a lot of work, in fact, he would have to rebuild the engine. She asked when he would finish the job so that she could get her car back. He said it would be done in about a week and towed the car to his shop. A week later, the son returned the car and presented Barbara with a bill for over $2,400. Barbara stared in disbelief and said, "But I am your mother! You can't charge your mother!" Ultimately, Carl took his mother to court, charging her with breach of contract.

Barbara argued that she had no contractual obligation because she never thought her son would charge her for helping his old mother and she never agreed to pay for the repairs. Carl's lawyer argued that an "implied contract" is created by the law any time that goods or services are requested by a buyer under circumstances in which people ordinarily expect to be paid.

What should the judge do in this mother/son situation? How should the law resolve the conflicting claims of Barbara and Carl? Does justice demand that we impose an "implied contract" on Barbara and make her pay the bill? Or is justice better served by forcing people to work for free for their mothers? Should there be any limits to that work? But before considering what the current law might say about this situation, we should first consider whether or not there is a "moral obligation" here. Does Barbara have a moral obligation to pay her son? Does Carl have a moral obligation to waive payment? The point is this: We are free to structure the "law" in any way that we believe is fair. In other words, the first purpose of law is to bring about justice and our own personal morality should form the basis of the laws we create.

Students typically split about even on what the "just" thing to do is in this case. Some are outraged at the son's claim. What kind of person would sue his own mother to recover compensation for services he rendered to help her out? Could she sue him for the cost of his Pampers? Or the tuition she paid for him to attend mechanic's school? Where does it end?

Others seem to take a more adversarial view. "Why should a struggling mechanic have to work for free on family cars? Could he charge his aunt? His rich cousin? The father who abandoned him at birth?" It is true, of course, that courts will enforce oral contracts, even when no one has agreed to "expressed terms." Have your gas tank filled in a service station or walk into a hair salon and get your hair cut and you have entered into an "implied contract." You have agreed to pay a reasonable amount for these goods or services. The law is clear: Any time someone accepts goods or services under circumstances in which an individual would reasonably expect to pay for them, the courts will enforce the contract. If you get into a cab and give an address, you cannot refuse to pay the cab fare by claiming that you thought the ride was free. On the other hand, if you accept a ride home from your friend and he presents you with a bill for his services, no court is going to enforce that "contract" and honor your friend's claim.

So where does that leave Barbara Fisher and her mechanic son? Is she "reasonable" in her belief that her loving son would never charge her for his services? Students often debate this issue with enthusiasm and always raise interesting arguments in support of their position. Occasionally, some will switch sides in midstream, having seen the light of the others' position. (This just could be the most valuable experience in these debates.)

When reasonable people disagree as to what justice demands as an outcome, we need the guidance of *stare decisis*, or legal precedent. How has the law dealt with this problem in the past? The precedent of the Anglo-American common law offers the thinking of some of the greatest legal minds in human history. The common law is almost 800 years old (having started with the signing of Magna Carta in 1215). What guidance can we get from those learned minds that have gone into forming the common law?

Along with the rules concerning implied contract, the common law contains a doctrine called the *presumption of gratuity*. The doctrine means that the law will presume that family members do not deal "at arm's length" and do not charge each other for household chores or little favors. For instance, when you put out the garbage or do the dishes for your family, you cannot claim an implied contract and sue your parents for compensation. Likewise, when you order a meal in a restaurant, you are going to have to pay a reasonable bill; but if you stop by mom's for dinner, you would not ordinarily be expected to pay. The law does not create an obligation to pay under circumstances in which reasonable people would believe the goods or services were free.

In the actual case of Barbara and Carl, the court examined the bill and found that about $1,400 of the bill was for parts that Carl had to buy in order to do the job. The other $1,000 was for Carl's labor in installing the parts. Ruling that the presumption of gratuity covered her son's labor only, the judge ordered Barbara to compensate her son for his out of pocket expenses, that is, the $1,400. But she did not have to pay for her son's labor since it was unreasonable for him to expect his mother to pay for his labor in the absence of an express contract.

He could have requested an agreement on her part to compensate him before the work began and the law would have respected that agreement. However, in the absence of such an express contract, he is not entitled to compensation for his labor. (It's likely Carl won't be celebrating Mother's Day for a while.)

A final question that arises from this case is the possibility of future modification of the presumption of gratuity. As the nature of family arrangements continues to change, more and more courts will face cases in which the lawsuit involves foster children living in the household or even children of a blended family where the parents have not actually married. Should the presumption of gratuity be extended to these situations? Would it be immoral to provide the same legal protection to these less traditional families?

This case, obviously, was an example of how common law doctrines can guide the thinking of judges and lawyers in trying to find the just thing to do. It is rare that students will immediately reach this same conclusion based on their "instincts for justice," and it is also the rare student who does not feel that justice was done in this case. So the limits on our sense of justice become apparent to the class, and the value of lawyers searching the precedent of the common law start to become clear.

Of course, in most cases the general principles of the common law created by judges are less important than specific statutes passed by legislatures. These statutes are created by political officials who have been elected based on their views of right and wrong; therefore, voters have a right to demand that these statutes reflect their own view of justice. However, once again students will disagree as to what constitutes justice in many of these situations.

For instance, the Uniform Commercial Code has been adopted by every state legislature. This code specifies the appropriate resolution to innumerable contractual disputes and these resolutions have been accepted by a majority of the state legislatures as just. Consider another example of a contract dispute that challenges our sense of justice:

Sale On Approval

Assume that you are thinking about buying one of the new high-definition televisions. The picture looks fabulous in the store, but $3,000 seems excessive. As you ponder the question of buying it or not, the salesperson at Macy's makes a suggestion. "Why not take it on a 'sale on approval' basis? If you don't like it, bring it back within thirty days and we will take it back, no hard feelings." You agree. You take it home. Everyone loves it. But after a few weeks, you start to feel a little buyer's remorse and you decide to return it to Macy's the next day—still within the thirty-day "sale on approval" period. That night a fierce thunder storm hits your neighborhood and a bolt of lightning comes through the window and hits the TV, sending it off to TV heaven.

The next morning, you call Macy's and tell them what a terrible thing has happened to *their* TV. Macy's legal department informs you that the TV is yours, and that if you are, for any reason, unable to return it intact, you are responsible for the $3,000 sale price. Is the legal department correct?

It is a matter of conjecture as to how students in the college classrooms of the sixties would have responded to this question, but it may be that the vast majority would have demanded that justice place the loss on the giant corporation rather than on the consumer. Today's students, on the other hand, usually split about evenly on this question, perhaps indicating a more benign view of capitalist corporations than the view held by their elders. About half of today's students responding to this question believe that justice requires that Macy's take the loss, while the others believe that the buyer should be held liable for the loss. How should this be resolved?

Actually, this is an important lesson for students to see firsthand the value of codified legal precedent. They have, at this point, expressed an opinion about justice that may well be diametrically opposed to that of the students sitting next to them. How should their difference of opinion be resolved? When reasonable people disagree about what constitutes justice, there really are just two options available. The first is the rule of law and the second is what Thomas Hobbes called the "law of tooth and claw"; in other words, the rule of violence. It would be possible for a society to design a system of adjudicating disputes like this wherein Macy's sends its biggest and toughest employee out to the parking lot to do battle with the buyer or the buyer's designated combatant. We could determine justice via combat (under the theory that might makes right). Or we could agree to abide by reasonable resolutions arrived at during the development of the common law. In the eight-century history of the English common law, great legal minds have wrestled again and again with problems that new students are confronting for the first time. Their efforts have been geared toward developing a system of laws that are best able to guide us to what they believe constitutes justice. A brief search in a law library to find out what legal precedent has to say about this kind of situation will reveal a section of the Uniform Commercial Code (UCC).

A look at a UCC section labeled "Sales on Approval" provides an insightful lesson on how precedent guides our thinking today. "In a sale on approval," it says, "no sale takes place until the buyer approves. Title and risk of loss remains with the seller until there is an approval." The law is clear and most lawyers should not need more than a few minutes to check the applicable law and inform the client about what to expect. Macy's takes the loss. That compilation of eight centuries of "technicalities," known as precedent or *stare decisis,* will resolve this contractual dispute quickly and peaceably. This is the value of having precedent to guide us in our search for justice.

In other areas of the law, however, there really is no precedent to guide our thinking. In these situations, judges must look to their own moral and political values for direction. If students pretend they are judges who are not bound by any law and told to "do the right thing" in a given case, the gap between the students' beliefs or positions becomes more apparent. For example, how far should the law allow government to go in regulating the behavior of individuals? When is a family decision no longer personal and private but part of a legitimate area of government regulation? When does government involvement in the life of the individual become "excessive" and therefore unjust? Consider the dilemma faced by a judge in Arkansas a few years ago:

Religious Objection To Medicine

Pamela Hamilton was a twelve-year-old girl who developed a malignant tumor on her hip. Since her parents were both fundamentalist Christians, they did not believe in modern medicine and they refused to have the child treated for her condition. The Reverend Larry Hamilton, Pamela's father, taught her that anyone who does not have enough faith in God to trust that God will take care of them will wind up in the eternal fires of hell.

The county Social Services Department took a somewhat more secular view. Hearing about Pamela's tumor, Social Services went to court and asked the judge to declare Pamela a ward of the court so that they could provide her with chemotherapy. The Hamiltons fought the request. They pointed to the horrors of chemotherapy, the chances that it would do no good anyway, and their right to practice their religion. Should the judge issue the order?

If the student were that Arkansas judge, what would she do? Should the order be issued? In cases like this, the judge cannot simply throw up her hands and say "I don't know!" The courtroom is full of people waiting for an answer and the judge must issue the order or refuse to issue the order. Students consistently split very close to evenly on this question, with about half agreeing to issue the court order. Does justice demand that Pamela be forcibly subjected to a program of chemotherapy, or should the court honor her parents' religious convictions and risk her death? Does government have the right to remove Pamela from her parents' care? Do the parents have the right, under the constitutionally guaranteed freedom of religion, to ignore the possible medical benefits of chemotherapy?

The debate on this issue frequently becomes very animated. Some students voice deeply felt moral convictions about freedom of religion and excessive government control. Others are appalled at the prospect of ignoring what they perceive as a case of child neglect. Those who see this case as a state encroachment on freedom of religion argue forcefully that the secular humanism of the government should not be given preferential treatment over the Hamiltons' deeply held beliefs. The others simply see this as a case of child neglect and always ask if the Hamiltons would also be allowed to let Pamela die of appendicitis. Invariably, there follows a discussion on the subject of parents who ignore the medical needs of their children for religious purposes. Should such behavior be condoned under the First Amendment? Should these parents be criminally prosecuted? Have their children taken away?

There are, of course, many gradations of this issue. The Bible says that Abraham heard an angel tell him to take his son Isaac to a mountaintop and slaughter him. In that case, the angel showed up again—just in time to stop the execution—but what should the law do to a modern-day Abraham whose angel shows up late? What about the religious group that includes poisonous snakes in their rituals? If one of their children is bitten and dies, should they be prosecuted?

A Boston district attorney faced a problem a few years back that illustrates this point. A Christian Science couple had watched and prayed as their young child suffered with appendicitis. While they were both college educated and knew appendicitis could be easily cured, their religion did not allow them to seek out modern medicine. The child's appendix ruptured after three or four days, peritonitis set in, and the child died an hour later. These facts were brought to the Boston DA, who had to decide whether or not this amounted to gross or criminal negligence on the part of the parents.

Students debate this point avidly, with the majority usually concluding that there should be no prosecution. But suppose we add an additional fact—a fact that has the benefit of being an actual part of the Boston case. It seems this was not the first child this couple had lost. Two years earlier, another one of their children had succumbed to peritonitis under similar conditions. What's more, they had another four children still at home who could face a similar risk. Should these children be taken away from them? Should they be arrested and prosecuted?

The additional facts generally change some minds and soften the views of the others. While we will postpone a discussion of the different levels of negligence until later, at this point students can see how addi-

tional information can easily change their opinion of the proper outcome. So what additional information would they like to have about
the Pamela Hamilton case?

Typically, someone will ask about the probabilities of the chemotherapy being effective. Actually, part of the value of this particular discussion is to give the class the opportunity to come up with the right
questions. In other words, what additional facts would the judge need
to have in order to make an informed decision?

One such piece of information has to do with the chances of success.
Clearly, if the chance of successfully forcing the tumor into remission is
one in a million, then there is less justification for governmental interference than in an appendicitis case where the odds of success are in the
99 percent range. The actual medical testimony at the Hamiltons'
court hearing suggested the chance of success of the chemo was about
25 percent. This new fact changes a few minds.

It is also argued that Pamela herself should be allowed to make the
decision. Clearly, were she an adult, no court would force her into
chemo against her will. But she is twelve years old with roughly normal
intelligence. Would we allow a seven-year-old to make such a decision?
Should the fact that she wants to do what her parents want her to do
make this any less a case of neglect?

The judge in the actual Hamilton case gave an inspiring little lecture
on the importance of freedom of religion, then granted the order and
sent Pamela off to the doctors. Always, in the classes that discuss
Pamela Hamilton, very close to half of each class disagrees with that decision. Most likely, half the population would disagree with the court's
decision as well.

At this point, some students will hold their ground and insist that
their own solution is more just. Clearly, the legal system cannot promise
an outcome that is perfectly just in every situation. It can only promise
an outcome that is as just as is humanly possible. It is important for students who are just beginning to study law to understand that point. We
are not computers. Our lives are complex and our relationships can
present situations that challenge our ability to render justice. Just as
certainly, students of other occupations can be encouraged to recognize that there can be more than one "right" way of viewing a situation.
In exploring the diversity of views expressed here, and the logic behind
them, it is possible to explore personal subjectivity, exposing such
thinking to the light and externalizing concepts of fairness.

CONSENSUS AND STANDPOINT EPISTEMOLOGY

There is little consensus on some of these questions and the law on the subject is currently evolving. In a free society, it is crucially important that this evolution follow the values of the people who are asked to obey that law. Respect for the law of a society generates political support for the regime that presides over it. Or, as it has more eloquently been phrased: "The strength of Rome lies not in her legions, but in her laws."

Thomas Jefferson argued that, in a democracy, the law should be a codification of the public's opinion. In the ideal democracy, the will of the majority should be reflected in the laws that are passed. Otherwise, in theory at least, the political leaders responsible for passing those laws will be replaced in the next election. Therefore, political leaders should consider public consensus about moral issues before voting in favor of a particular piece of legislation.

Which laws we tend to favor or oppose very often depends on what our political viewpoint is. In turn, where we "stand" on political issues very often depends on where we "sit" in life. For example, if a Gallup poll asks a thousand respondents what they think should be done about the minimum wage and the capital gains tax, we can pretty well predict the responses if we know in advance the life circumstances of the respondents. People who are living on a minimum wage are more likely to favor an increase in that wage, as well as an increase in the capital gains tax, which they are not likely to be subject to. Likewise, those who live on gains from capital investments are very likely to believe that the capital gains tax is already too high.

It is human nature to be biased in favor of laws that favor people like ourselves. And it is very important to analyze the influence of our own "standpoint" on the conclusions we reach about the fairness of a proposed law. Professor John Rawls suggested in *Theory of Justice* that students should try to imagine themselves in a society in which they did not know their own social position or personal assets. In other words, if they had no idea where they would be positioned in society (rich, poor, educated, illiterate, black, white, etc.), what kinds of laws would they favor in order to create a "just society"?

This experiment is very useful in helping students to understand how where they stand politically depends significantly on where they sit in life.

Others can use such a discussion as an introduction to connecting issues of values clarification to personal situations. To students of education, for example, such a discussion can be a self-awareness exercise exploring values, which may unwittingly intrude into relationships with parents who may "sit" in very different life circumstances than their own.

The passing of the years, moreover, can change one's viewpoint of what constitutes justice. Consider the problem faced by a probate judge when the justice of a Last Will and Testament is challenged:

Leaving Assets to Loved Ones

John and Agnes were married for fifty years. John gave Agnes a minuscule household budget that she could barely get by on, but he managed to accumulate $100,000 in a bank account in his own name. At this point, John met a nineteen-year-old named Brittany. Smitten beyond words, John left town on the back of Brittany's Harley-Davidson and a month later John is found dead of a heart attack in a motel room in Las Vegas. In his pocket is a Last Will and Testament. "To my loving wife, Agnes," the will says, "who always wanted to be mentioned in my will, 'Hi, Agnes!' And to Brittany, a young lady who has made my life so joyous over the past month, I leave my $100,000."

What does justice demand in this case? Should the probate court honor John's expressed desire with regard to the disposition of his assets? Should the will be set aside and Brittany disinherited?

Female student attitudes toward this problem offer a good example of "standpoint epistemology." Older females have tended to be overwhelmingly sympathetic to the long-term wife. "Agnes has earned that money," they argue. "Justice demands that Agnes get that money." Younger students side with Brittany in much larger numbers.

"It's John's money," they insist. "He can do what he wants with it." After discussing the fairness of both viewpoints, students are informed that almost all states have something like an estate power trust law, which provides for the disinherited wife and offers her the opportunity to "elect against the will" and receive her statutory share—generally 50 percent of the estate. So, in this case, Agnes would get $50,000 and Brittany the rest, and we would declare that "justice" had been done.

CONCLUSION

Through processes such as these, students have an opportunity to learn that the function of law is to guide us in our search for justice and that the concept of what constitutes justice is not something that we all agree upon. They also see examples of how our own moral values figure prominently in determining what we mean by justice and what kinds of laws we would support. Should parents have to pay for the professional services supplied by their grown children? Should the courts be empowered to take sick children away from parents who were not doing all they could to provide them with the most modern medical care?

When a moral consensus can be found among the public concerning the social problems of the day, the next question is how to structure reasonable laws that are rationally related to dealing with those problems. Underlying every law should be some logical rationale for the goals it seeks to achieve. In other words, as we shall see in Chapter 2, every rule should have a reason.

SUGGESTED READINGS

Greene, M. (1978). Wide-awakeness and the moral life. In *Landscapes of learning* (pp. 42–52). New York: Teachers College Press.

Levi, E.H. (1962). *Introduction to legal reasoning*. Chicago: University of Chicago Press.

O'Connell, J. & Bell, P.A. (1997). *Accidental justice: The dilemmas of tort law*. New Haven: Yale University Press.

Rawls, J. (1999). *A theory of justice*. Cambridge: Bellnap Press.

Scheck, B., Neufeld, P., & Dwyer, J. (2000). *Actual innocence*. New York: Doubleday.

Vygotsky, L.S. (1978). *Mind in society: The development of higher psychological processes*. Cambridge, MA: Harvard University Press. (Original work published in 1930, 1933, 1935)

Chapter 2

The Logic of the Law

> While making law and making sausages may turn our stomachs, there is at least supposed to be an underlying logic in legislation.

It has been suggested by some educational psychologists that today's students—at all levels, but certainly including college students—actually learn in a somewhat different way from earlier generations. The cause of this, they argue, is the massive exposure of today's students to the electronic media during their early socialization, an exposure that has, for the most part, replaced exposure to the written word, which earlier generations had experienced.

Consider what happens to two young children learning about the same event from different sources, say, George Washington cutting down the cherry tree. The first reads the story in a book; the second watches a video. The first child follows the linear logic of the printed word. He absorbs each word, each sentence, and each paragraph; he stumbles over new or difficult words; rereads sentences that are not clear upon first reading. His brain fills in graphic images that are provoked by the words. Each word group draws a picture that grows out of the imagination and the thinking process.

The second child watches a video about George and the cherry tree and is much more passive in experiencing the story. Pictures and sounds create a mosaic to be observed, to be experienced. Instead of the linear logic of the printed word, she picks up visual impressions, sometimes subliminal, as the facts of the story are acted out instantaneously. The details of the story blend into the colors and the voices and the music. In the end, her memory of the story is different from his. In short, the learning experiences of the two students are very different.

Today's college students "know" things in a somewhat different way from the way in which their grandparents "knew" things, and, to a lesser extent, from the way their parents "know" things. And much of the difference has to do with logic. Logic is at the heart of the law. Students who are taking introductory courses in law need to be exposed to some fundamental concepts, which are necessary to an understanding of the law and political system that uses the law to govern.

Beginning law students are frequently reminded that after three years of study they will never think the same way again. Naturally, they can expect to be older and wiser and poorer—and used to working harder than ever before—but they will also think differently. What that means, however, is that the most important change they will experience during the next three years is not the accumulation of an enormous amount of information about case law and statutes and the legal process. The most important difference is that as lawyers, they will never again think through a question the way nonlawyers do.

This proves to be correct. Lawyers do think differently. The "logic of the law" forces the law student to start viewing intellectual problems in a new way. The challenge is to stay on point, that is, keep your eye on the issue. Follow the logic of the argument step by step and avoid the temptation to stray off onto some related issue—which may be interesting or controversial or current—but which takes the argument into irrelevant territory.

"Relevance" is the key issue. Students of law as well as the most seasoned judges always have to ask themselves: "Does this fact that I am about to introduce to the discussion bear a reasonable relationship to the issue at hand?" It seems to college professors today that one of the greatest distinctions that can be made between the college students of earlier generations and those of today has to do with this ability to follow the logic of an argument. Earlier generations were certainly not all gifted logicians nor are all of today's students incapable of logical discourse. However, the brain that is educated by a bombardment of audio and video impressions seems to be more easily distracted from the issue at hand than the brains of those whose early socialization was primarily guided by the printed word.

"Rules of law," says John Dewey, "are in fact the institution of conditions under which persons make their arrangements with one another."[1] While the logic of the law may seem to pertain to the study of certain disciplines more than others, perhaps such limited focus does our youth a disservice. Teachers at all levels could benefit from learning to think rationally and to teach rationality. The concept of *democracy* rests on the ability of citizens to understand and articulate its value and on their deligence in defending against its diminishment. Such skills take time and attention to develop. Although most of us would hope that individual families could accomplish this task, we recognize that in a democracy, every voter's education is essential to us all. It is to teachers that we, as a nation, have entrusted the work of helping students learn to think responsibly and in a fashion that will allow our way of life to continue.

In a world where the media is increasingly becoming the message, the future of our democracy may rest as never before on the infusion of new generations of thinking Americans. Such citizens should be able to understand the logic of political and other arguments, should be able to distinguish the relevant facts in a discussion, and should be interested in seeking out the reasoning by which our laws can respond to the evolving values and concepts of justice on which our social contract rests.

Unfortunately, such a focus is becoming even less apparent as more and more of our elementary and high schools cave in to the press for "accountability." Instead of helping young people learn to think, school administrators are turning to a growing emphasis on "covering" material that can be measured through standardized testing. This process seems to satisfy many who have the power to sway public opinion, but does little to produce the thinking, the understanding, and the meaning-making which are the hallmarks of those educated persons who will be capable of making the complex moral decisions which the future will demand of our citizens.

Theodore and Nancy Sizer, in their book, *The Students Are Watching: Schools and the Moral Contract*, use the term "grappling" to describe the painstaking mental process by which students learn to construct the meaning "of one's immediate condition against a sweep of human and environmental experience, past and present. . . . Important matters of sensitive living," they conclude, "have everything to do with hard, substantive, and often agonizingly painful thought."[2]

Increasing numbers of schoolpeople, according to the Sizers, are aware that a curriculum which presents "a watery diet of . . . absolutes as a way to avoid conflict" will not produce the moral development we hope for in our youth. These schoolpeople recognize that "the moral is embedded in the intellectual, that thinking hard—grappling—in an informed and careful way is the most likely route to a principled and constructive life."[3]

It is wise for today's professors to go out of their way to spend a good deal of time in class giving examples that demand a certain adherence to principles of deductive reasoning. A few examples of the "logic of the law" will help make this point. These examples will include the basic legal concepts dealing with the laws governing negligence, personal property, and alibis.

Child Neglect or Meddling Do-Gooder?

In Florida a few years ago, a man left a two-year-old baby alone in his car when he ran into a post office. The baby, caught in the summer heat inside the locked car began to cry and a Good Samaritan passing by came to the child's aid. When the father returned to his car, he found his window had been smashed, his baby removed from the car and a small crowd had gathered to help "save the baby." When the police arrived, the father demanded that the "kidnapper" be arrested for smashing the window of his car and stealing his child. The "rescuer" and the crowd demanded that the police arrest the father for child neglect.

Students usually divide on this issue with great enthusiasm. Four out of five will condemn the irresponsible father, praise the Good Samaritan and sympathize with the sweltering baby. However, if the facts are presented in just a slightly different way, a majority will swing to the father's side. It rapidly becomes apparent that each side has made assumptions about the case, which may or may not be true.

The questions then become: What additional information do we need in order to analyze this situation thoroughly and assess culpability? What additional "relevant evidence" concerning time span and temperature and other circumstances should be gathered? And what standard will the law use to establish that culpability?

The concept of "negligence" is a very important part of both civil and criminal law. The logic that undergirds negligence law is a good way for beginning students to be exposed to the logic of the law. Juries may disagree sometimes about whether or not a particular form of behavior constitutes negligence, but the judge in the trial will attempt to explain to them the standards by which we evaluate human behavior to determine if it rises to the level of negligence.

The all-important standard that the jury will hear about is the "reasonable person test." The jury will be asked to determine what the theoretical "reasonable person" would have done in this particular situation. Take the baby out of the car seat and carry him into the post office? Suppose there was a heavy rain falling and the father only had to go twenty feet away from the car for less than a minute?

Should the "rescuer" have waited until the police arrived before smashing the window? Suppose he did wait for five minutes, the outside temperature was in the nineties, the temperature inside the car was probably over a hundred, and the baby appeared to be losing consciousness? What would the reasonable person do? Did the actions of the father measure up to the "reasonable person test"?

An important part of negligence is the question of "foreseeability." Given the totality of the circumstances known to the father at the time he left the baby alone in that car, was the danger to the baby "foreseeable" to the reasonable person? At what point does the danger of harm become foreseeable to a reasonable person? The law will not punish an individual for damages that result from his actions if the danger was totally unforeseeable. Say, for example, a meteorite strikes and kills your companion while walking through a park that you suggested walking through. Since you had no way of foreseeing this event you cannot be held liable for the harm done to the victim. On the other hand, let's suppose you had suggested a stroll through a minefield. "Foreseeability" is the key that gives the "proximate causation" necessary to establish negligence. Consider an example of foreseeability that students invariably understand:

The Dog Bite

Alice and Betty each had a guest to their individual homes for dinner. Their respective guests sue both Alice and Betty because of injuries incurred when a pet belonging to their host attacked them. Alice's dinner guest, Alvin, was attacked by Alice's pit bull as he walked toward the dining room table. He was the seventh dinner guest attacked by this dog in the past year. Is Alice liable for the damage done to her guest?

Betty did not have a pit bull. She had a pet gold fish and it was the gold fish that caused the injury to Betty's dinner guest, Bob. Betty watched in horror as the fish went into some kind of frenzy in his bowl, raced in concentric circles around the bowl until he built up sufficient momentum to launch a suicide attack on the jugular vein on the neck of Betty's guest. Zoologists testify that this is the first time in the history of the species that such an assault has been observed among gold fish.

Students sense immediately that Alice should be held liable for the damages done to her dinner guest while Betty should not. Clearly, "foreseeability" is a pivotal issue in these situations. If the damage done is not reasonably foreseeable to the defendant, then there should be no liability.

In the most renowned negligence case in American legal history, *Palsgraff v. the Long Island Railroad*, Justice Cardozo wrote the immortal words: "The danger to be perceived defines the care to be observed." Since the danger of the pit-bull attack was obviously foreseeable and the danger of the gold fish attack obviously was not, Alice will pay, Betty will not. Such is the logic of the law.

Would it not be morally wrong to impose any different standard? Since the attack of the gold fish is not foreseeable, Betty is not morally responsible for the damage. To hold someone *legally* liable for something for which she is not *morally* responsible is clearly unjust. Every attempt is made in the Anglo-American common law to tie together concepts of moral guilt and legal liability.

Likewise, making every negligent act a criminal act is also unjust. We are only human. We make mistakes. The vast majority of these mistakes will result in civil negligence lawsuits, but not be prosecuted as crimes. To reach a level of *criminal negligence,* the circumstances must indicate an extreme form of carelessness known as *gross negligence.*

GROSS NEGLIGENCE

How far can negligent behavior go before the law will impose criminal liability on a defendant, rather than just civil liability? In the above example, suppose Alice's guest Alvin was killed by that pit bull. Will Alice be prosecuted for criminal homicide, in addition to being sued for compensatory damages? Suppose the baby in the overheated car had died when the father did not return and there had been no Good Samaritan?

The law attempts to connect moral failure to legal ramifications as closely as possible. In other words, the law should punish behavior that is considered morally outrageous, more than the law should punish what is considered just slightly wrong. To the extent that it is possible, we try to connect the idea of "liability," which is a legal concept, to the idea of "fault," which is a moral concept. Criminal liability will not ordinarily attach until behavior has reached the level of "gross negligence."

To reduce this concept to its most rudimentary form, consider the proper reaction to the driver of a car that kills a child. One driver is doing 56 miles per hour in a 55 zone; the other driver is doing 105 miles per hour in the same zone. Should the legal ramifications be the same? Both have killed a child. Both have broken the law. But, clearly, the moral culpability is totally different and so should be the legal punishment.

The law distinguishes between "ordinary negligence" and "gross negligence." Gross negligence is criminal negligence and can lead to a felony conviction. The judge will tell the jury that gross negligence is simply "an extreme form of ordinary negligence," and if they find that the defendant's action constituted an extreme form of ordinary negligence, then they may convict the defendant of a felony.

Clearly, the driver who accidentally kills a child while doing 105 MPH in a 55 zone is guilty of the kind of gross negligence that will justify a conviction of manslaughter. But suppose there was even worse negligence. Suppose the driver was doing 105 MPH, but he was also drunk and driving on a crowded street where children were playing. Are there not some situations where logic demands that we make further distinctions between forms of negligence? Should this driver be treated the same way as the driver doing 105 on an interstate highway?

The law acknowledges that there are some forms of human negligence that are so outrageous as to warrant even greater punishment. We call it "recklessness"—an extreme form of gross negligence. And in most jurisdictions if a jury looks at the "totality of the circumstances" and concludes that the defendant acted with a "reckless disregard for a known risk to human life," the conviction will be not for manslaughter—punishable usually by about three or four years actually served in prison—but rather for second-degree murder, punished far more severely. Again, such is the logic of the law.

RECKLESSNESS

Gross negligence is a standard that is also used in some situations dealing with defamation of character. The tort of *libel* consists of making an untrue statement that subjects the victim to hatred, scorn, ridicule, or social disgrace. The damages that are awarded in a successful defamation of character lawsuit will often be *punitive damages* as opposed to simple *compensatory damages.*

Compensatory damages are defined as the amount of money that is determined by the jury to put the plaintiff back into the position he would have been in had the defendant not harmed him in the first place. In its simplest form, if an auto accident results in $500 worth of damage to the plaintiff's car and the jury rules that the defendant was responsible for the accident, the "compensatory damages" will be set at $500. It is likely that the jury may also rule that the plaintiff is entitled to other ancillary expenses such as the cost of a rented car to replace his own car while it is being repaired. In a defamation action the compensatory damages will be the amount of money a plaintiff lost because his reputation was harmed and the jury's estimate of how much the embarrassment of the defamation is worth.

Unlike compensatory damages, *punitive damages* seek to punish the defendant for libeling or slandering the victim in cases where compensatory damages may not be appropriate for achieving such a goal. For instance, when Carol Burnett successfully sued the *National Enquirer*, the jury found that she had not suffered any actual economic losses because of the defamatory article. In fact, the jury concluded that since virtually no one actually believes what they read in the *National Enquirer*, Carol Burnett was not likely to lose any fans or future professional opportunities because of the article.

So, should the court simply award Ms. Burnett "nominal damages," usually $1, which would give her the satisfaction of having won her case but in no way discourage the defendant from publishing such articles? Obviously, the law should provide some additional punishment. When students are questioned about what punishment they feel is morally appropriate in such a case, their answers vary widely. The more Draconian suggest putting the *National Enquirer* out of business or jailing the editors. The more forgiving students suggest that a front-page retraction might be sufficient.

The jury in the actual case awarded Carol Burnett $1 in nominal damages and $1.5 million in punitive damages. (She gave it to charity.)

It was a way of getting the attention of the editors at the *National Enquirer* and prompting them to be more careful in their future stories.

But a problem arises when newspapers are sued for minor mistakes or oversights. The potential financial losses may force newspapers to hold back on publishing important stories, which the public has a right to hear about. It would be an unfortunate situation if editors were constantly fearful about publishing information they had received from whistle blowers if their legal departments were obsessively peering over their shoulders. If every minor mistake of fact could lead to bankruptcy, the media coverage of important stories would indeed become very unsatisfactory. The American dedication to a free press is so great that the law has been logically structured to preclude this situation.

In order to prevent news sources from facing bankruptcy for minor mistakes, the law provides a "conditional privilege" to publishers of newspapers and the electronic media. In essence, the privilege requires that before a judgment can be entered against a newspaper for defamation, the plaintiff must prove to the jury that the defendant either deliberately lied about the victim (which is very rare) or was *grossly negligent* in gathering the facts of the story. In other words, ordinary negligence is not enough, the plaintiff must prove gross negligence. The result is that it is very difficult to prevail in a defamation suit against a newspaper and our "free press"—some would say *too* free—is protected against an abundance of defamation suits.

Carol Burnett's case, however, faced not just the difficulty of the newspaper's conditional privilege. It also had to overcome the "public figure rule." In order to maximize the freedom that newspapers have in covering public figures, the law provides additional protection to stories concerning them. In essence, a defamation lawyer representing a public figure in most states must prove to the jury that the defendant's conduct not only went beyond the level of negligence, but that it went beyond the level of gross negligence as well. The standard of "recklessness" is used to measure the paper's behavior.

Defamation lawyers discourage most celebrities from suing a newspaper because of this public figure rule. The lawyers explain that the public figure rule requires that they prove *recklessness* in the gathering of the facts before a judgment can be won and that it is almost impossible to establish recklessness.

In the Burnett case, however, the facts were so outrageous that she insisted on taking a shot at the jury. The article published by the *Enquirer* claimed that Burnett had become drunk in a Washington restaurant and had gotten involved in an altercation with Henry Kissinger.

The truth was that both Burnett and Kissinger were in the restaurant that night but not simultaneously. He arrived about two hours after she had left. She was not drunk—she does not drink at all, because her parents had been alcoholics.

So how did they gather the facts for this story? The *Enquirer* reporters often pass out their cards in restaurants that celebrities frequent. They offer employees financial rewards if they can use a story that they phone in to the paper. In the Burnett case, a busboy who spoke no English had called an editor in Los Angeles. The editor spoke no Spanish. Somehow the editor picked up a few nebulous facts and simply winged it from there.

The jury found that this was more than "negligent." It was more than "grossly negligent." It amounted to "recklessness" and it overcame the conditional privilege offered by the law to protect a free press against defamation suits from public figures.

PERSONAL PROPERTY

In many cases, students choose where they would like to sit on the first day of each semester and, for the most part, they sit in the same desks throughout the semester. They seem to think of them as "their desks" and other students ordinarily honor their claims and would not think of sitting at another's desk. It can be interesting to question them about this phenomenon.

Do they "own" the desks? Could they take them home at the end of the semester as a little souvenir of the course? Could they sell their rights to sit there to another student—rights that seem to be informally established among themselves? If they have another class in this room, can they enforce their right to sit at the same desks?

As a way of demonstrating the logic of the law with regard to personal property (essentially any property that is movable and therefore not "real" property), the student needs to distinguish between three distinct legal concepts: *custody, possession* and *title.*

"Custody" is the right to hold on to a piece of personal property, usually to protect it from others until the owner returns. Usually referred to by lawyers as "mere custody," this is the right that a coat check person gets when you check you coat. Or the right given to hold your car in a Park and Lock lot.

"Possession" is the right to both take custody of personal property and to exercise acts of discretion with regard to the property. Possession may not be "90 percent of the law," as the saying goes, but it is a very important concept in law. You cannot be convicted of stealing a piece of personal property that you do not own but are in legal possession of. And you *can* be convicted of stealing personal property that you, in fact, own if someone else is entitled to legal possession of it at the time. So possession is very important.

If I park and lock my car in your parking lot, you do not have the right to drive it. Or lend it to a friend. Or exercise any other actions which an owner would be entitled to. This is because you have "mere custody" of my car. However, if I lend you my car, I have given you "possession." You may drive it, wash it, add oil to it, or even transfer possession of it to another. In other words, you may exercise discretion over the property.

"Ownership" is the third legal relationship an individual can have with property. It means that the individual holds legal title to the property. People may have all three types of relationship at the same moment. They have "custody" of their desk; they may have "possession" of a borrowed pen; and they have "title" to their notebook. With this as background, consider the problem of who is entitled to possess property that had been stolen and sold to a good-faith purchaser.

Fraud versus Theft

When Bob's new job provides him with a new laptop computer, he decides to sell his old one. He advertises it in the paper and Al responds with an offer of $400, which Bob accepts. Al pays with a personal check, which Al knows is no good because he closed the account a month ago. By the time Bob finds out that Al's check is no good, Al has sold the laptop to Carol, a good-faith purchaser, without notice that the computer was stolen.

If the students again assume that they are a judge hearing this case and authorized by the state law to simply "do the right thing," how would they rule? In the ideal world, everybody will get their property back; that is, Al will give back the $400 to Bob and Carol will get to keep the laptop. But in the real world, we all know that Al has probably invested that money in controlled substances and no one is ever going to squeeze $400 out of him. So, who takes the loss? Bob or Carol?

Students all agree that justice demands that Al be punished for his act of fraud. But when it comes to deciding who gets the computer, students generally seem to sense that the it should stay with Carol, though they are never quite sure why. However, when the facts are changed just slightly, a consensus about the "just solution" emerges. If Al had been a burglar rather than a con man, students seem to sense that some pivotal issue has changed. Should Carol—still a good-faith purchaser—get to keep the computer when Al acquired it through a burglary of Bob's home? Or should Bob get his property back? The overwhelming vote by the students is that, in the case of burglary, the original owner should get his property back from the good-faith purchaser, even though the purchaser should be allowed to keep the property in the case where it was acquired by fraud. They sense that this is the "just solution." But rarely can anyone explain how the law can make a logical distinction that will allow for this outcome.

The students' instincts in this case are legally correct. The logic of the law is clear: A seller of personal property can transfer no more "title" than he has. A burglar simply takes possession of the property while title stays with the victim. The law, however, will honor the intention of the owner of property that is transferred pursuant to a fraudulent transaction. So when Bob gives the laptop to Al, even though the check is no good and Al is guilty of fraud, it is Bob's intention to transfer title to Al. The law will respect Bob's intention. Al has title to the laptop when he leaves Bob and he is therefore legally able to transfer title to Carol. In other words, while only possession passes to the burglar, both possession and title pass to the thief in the case of fraud. Such is the logic of the law.

ALIBI

The Latin term for the word "elsewhere" is *alibi*. When a criminal defendant raises the defense of "alibi" he is arguing that at the time of the offense he was somewhere other than at the crime scene and he could not, therefore, have committed the crime. Ordinarily, the defendant will seek to establish his defense by bringing in the testimony of alibi witnesses, often a weeping wife who swears that he was home with her all night.

The Look-Alike Criminal

While Alan is taking a walk by himself on the beach, a convenience store in his neighborhood is held up by an individual who could pass for his twin. The store clerk identifies Alan; he is arrested by the police and charged with armed robbery. He is facing seven years in prison. Witnesses swear that Alan was the perpetrator. Alan was alone on the beach and he saw no one during his forty-five-minute walk. Alan's lawyer says he cannot shake the story of the eyewitnesses but that the DA will plea bargain if he will accept a three-year sentence.

How many students would consider accepting the plea bargain? After considering their options, at least half the students agree to the plea bargain and state that they would plead guilty to a crime they had not committed. They argue that they would probably make parole in a year and a half and that is a lot less than seven years. And you have to listen to your lawyers, don't you?

But how many of them could find someone to lie under oath for them and swear that they were with them on the beach? Can they find someone who would be an "alibi witness" and perjure themselves under oath by swearing that they had also been on that beach at the time of the crime? About four out of five students indicate that they could probably find such a volunteer. They feel that they actually do know someone who loves them enough to risk a conviction for perjury in order to keep them out of prison. (It would probably be worthwhile for the other one-fifth of the class to check out their lives and the nature of their relationships!)

A young law student in New York worked as a law clerk after school and experienced firsthand the ease with which an alibi can be created. The clerk's boss was a lawyer defending a counterfeiter. The Treasury agents alleged that their client had been in a bar in Brooklyn when an agent came in to meet with him. They had gone outside and exchanged counterfeit money for cash from the agent. The agents then went into the bar and arrested their client. The government's case had problems with it. The agents were running late that day and they had failed to mark the buy money. They were also supposed to videotape the transaction but they could not find a parking spot in front of the bar and the camera was too far away to see anything. The lawyer had a fairly good chance of creating a reasonable doubt in the mind of the jury.

During the week-long trial, the law clerk was alone in the office late one afternoon. A middle-aged man came into the office to discuss the case. He claimed to be a friend of the client and to have been with him in the bar that night. The clerk asked if he had been there when the agent came in to talk to the client and he said that no one had come in, that the client had never left the bar and that he was willing to testify to this.

The law clerk was elated. This would certainly help the case. This was direct evidence of the client's innocence. And then the man said, "I want $1,500 for my testimony." The clerk said *goodbye* and ushered him out of the office. He had received his first lesson in the ease with which alibi evidence can be created.

So, how can the law deal with this situation? How can a prosecutor ever prevent a defendant from creating a reasonable doubt by producing a reasonably credible alibi witness? If four out of five average college students—hardly career criminals—can find a loved one ready to swear under oath that their alibi is true and that they are therefore not guilty, how can prosecutors ever get convictions in cases where alibi is a plausible defense?

The answer that the law has evolved is to allow the judge to caution the jury in a special way about the defense of alibi. The judge will typically encourage the jurors to carefully scrutinize alibi testimony and weigh the credibility of the alibi witness. Did she have a reason to lie about the defendant's whereabouts? Did she offer any corroboration to her statement? In most states, judges will explain the ease with which an alibi can be created and in many jurisdictions judges are authorized to tell the jury that the "standard of proof" for alibi is not the usual "preponderance of the evidence" but the more demanding "clear and convincing evidence." In other words, if jurors do not feel that the defense has established an alibi by "clear and convincing evidence," they are free to disregard the alibi altogether.

The difference may seem obscure at first blush, but the difference is real and can be helpful to a juror who is seeking the truth. If a "preponderance of the evidence" can be thought of as 51 percent of the evidence, and if evidence "beyond a reasonable doubt" can be thought of as 95 percent of the evidence, then "clear and convincing evidence" should be thought of as about 75 percent of the evidence. In other words, if the juror feels that on the issue of alibi, the "weeping wife" may have offered a "preponderance of the evidence" as to the whereabouts of her husband at the time of the offense but not "clear and convincing evidence," then the juror is authorized by the judge to ignore the alibi evidence altogether. So while very strong alibi evidence is still enough to result in an acquittal, not every defendant with a friend who will perjure himself is going to go free. Once more we can see that such is the logic of the law.

CONCLUSION

There are times when the law may fall behind social realities and appear to be illogical in some areas but the law is probably not really the "ass and the idiot" that the Dickens character Uriah Heep claimed it to be. Most principles of the common law are based on the very solid logic of the great minds that went into fashioning our legal precedent. Whether it is in distinguishing between *negligence* and *gross negligence* or between *possession* and *title* or between a *preponderance of the evidence* and *clear and convincing evidence*, the law seeks to make logical classifications that will guide our thinking and help us arrive at a just conclusion.

Students who learn the logic of such distinctions in decision making can utilize the same principles in their own lives and work. Teachers, for example, deal with issues of ethics on a daily basis. Learning to reflect on these issues in an objective manner is an essential component of fairness. Yet, emotions sometimes unwittingly cloud fair judgment. While logic does not preclude the need for emotion and sensitivity in such decision making, its use can encourage the teacher, and anyone who deals with children and families, to look at both sides of a problem without assuming that her own stance is automatically correct. Such an approach is especially appropriate when the sounding board of people with decision-making power consists of others in like positions.

Of course, times change. Laws based on our understanding of the human experience as it was 500 years ago would be inadequate to guide us today. As times change and social realities change, the law must also change. The process by which the law changes will be taken up in Chapter 3.

NOTES

1. J. Dewey, *The public and its problems* (Athens, OH: Swallow Press, 1954), 54. (Original work published in 1927)
2. T. Sizer & N. Sizer, *The students are watching: Schools and the moral contract* (Boston, MA: Beacon Press, 1999), 23.
3. Ibid., 38.

SUGGESTED READINGS

Glannon, J. (2000). *The law of torts.* New York: Panel Publishing.

Kadish, S. N., & Schulhofer, S. (1998). *Criminal law and its processes: Cases and materials.* New York: Little Brown & Co.

Kionka, E.J. (1999). *Torts in a nutshell: Examples and explanation.* St. Paul, MN: West Publishing.

McGurt, B. (1997). *America's court: The Supreme Court and the people.* Golden, CO: Fulcrum Publishing.

Prosser, W.L., Wade, J.W., & Schwartz, V.E. (1994). *Cases and materials on torts.* (9th ed.). Mineola, NY: Foundation Press.

Chapter 3

Change in the Law

Stability is a very desirable characteristic in any legal system. The law should provide the security of consistent results so that an individual's behavior will result in predictable legal consequences. The law should not be changed lightly, but there are always changes in social realities that demand legal reforms. As a way of introducing the idea of changes in the law, consider the following hypothetical example.

The Pot-Smoking Abortionist

A federal prosecutor in New York got on a plane to Washington, DC. She was going to Washington in order to prosecute a criminal case against a doctor who was accused of both performing an abortion as well as smoking marijuana. The prosecutor joked with the flight attendant about "hijacking" the plane as she lit up a Marlboro.

How will the law treat these events if the year in which they happened was 1950 or 2000?

Today's students find it hard to believe that abortionists were routinely imprisoned in the fifties, and almost impossible to believe that some state penal codes of the fifties provided life in prison for smoking marijuana. For the most part, they also do not remember a time when smoking cigarettes on planes was permitted or when joking about hijacking a plane was not a federal offense.

There is a *maxim of law* that deals with when the law should change. A maxim of law is not really a law at all but rather a kind of guiding principle in legal reasoning. "Ignorance of the law is no excuse" is an example of a maxim. All states have adopted various maxims of law that have developed and evolved over the 800-year history of the common law. One of the most important maxims of law has to do with when the law should change. Maxims are generally written in Latin—perhaps to emphasize their importance, or maybe just to give lawyers yet another little secret that will help them justify their fees. *Cessante ratione legis, cessat ipsa lex* is a maxim, which translates as: "When the reason for the law ceases, the law itself should cease."

In other words, every rule should have a reason. There should be some underlying rationale for each law in order to justify its existence and if things should change so that the rationale no longer exists, the law should be changed. For instance, three-year-old Nolan wants to know why he has to eat his spinach and why he has an eight o'clock bedtime. His mother explains the rationale for both rules in terms of his youth and inability to decide for himself what is in his own best interest.

Close the scene; open it again three decades later. Nolan complains to his mom that he is the only thirty-three-year-old on the block who has to eat his spinach and be in bed by eight. The underlying rationale that had previously justified the rule no longer exists. If his mother spoke Latin, Nolan might tell her, *Cessante ratione legis, cessat ipsa lex.*

Of course, as the world changes, so too do rationales. There was a time when U.S. federal law actually provided substantial subsidies for the tobacco industry. Tobacco was assumed to be a harmless commodity that provided pleasure, profits, and jobs. Then the surgeon general discovered the evils of tobacco and the law was changed. More knowledge about a subject frequently dissolves the underlying rationale for various laws. Consider the "year and a day rule":

Sometime in the fourteenth century, the English decided that no one could be charged with murder if his victim lived for a year and a day after the assault. The reason for the law was medical ignorance. In other words, medical knowledge at the time was so limited that no one could say for sure that the victim's death was actually caused by the blow that had been struck so long ago. It was considered unfair to punish a defendant for the death of an individual who may have died from causes other than the assault committed by the defendant.

As medical science developed over the centuries, doctors were able to determine with more and more medical certainty whether or not the original blow had caused the death. Accordingly, the "year and a day rule" was gradually phased out of Anglo-American law. When the reason for the rule ceased, the rule itself also ceased.

MEDICAL TECHNOLOGY AND THE LAW

The question of justice is nowhere more intense than when we are dealing with the subject of human life. As the twenty-first century begins, the pace of change in medical technology overwhelms legal doctrines that are centuries old. The need for the law to acknowledge these changes and to make appropriate adjustments becomes obvious from one news story to the next.

Questions concerning when human life begins and when we should be allowed to terminate it are among the most profound moral quandaries of our era. During the last twenty-five years, the U.S. Supreme Court has handed down decisions involving abortion, the death penalty, and euthanasia. Each case had dissenting opinions. Little wonder, then, that there is less than unanimity on these issues in college classrooms.

Today's students seem to hold opinions about these issues that are substantially different from those of their parents' generation. Oddly enough, when the subject is either abortion or the death penalty, the change in view appears to be in opposite directions, depending on the method of terminating life that is under discussion. Most abortions performed in the sixties were still criminal offenses in the penal codes of most states, and college students of the day were accustomed to seeing abortionists arrested, prosecuted, and imprisoned. Few college students—or professors—in those days spoke of a woman's "right to choose" or of a constitutional right to terminate a pregnancy. In 1973, all that changed with the Supreme Court decision in *Roe v. Wade*.

While many of today's students still believe that abortion is morally wrong and should be limited or even treated as a criminal offense, clearly there has been a massive shift in opinion to the left on this issue. Today's students are more accepting of abortion than their parents were.

Equally massive has been the shift in the opposite direction on the issue of the death penalty. The fear of crime that pervades the American public and the frustration with our inability to "do something" about violent crime have changed the prevailing view of capital punishment. Today's college students are, by and large, supportive of the death penalty in far greater numbers than their parents' generation was during their college days. But the arguments favoring or opposing abortion or the death penalty are so well worn that many of these arguments sound platitudinous. The level of the debate bounces around with bumper-sticker arguments and neither side seems to hear the other's view. It is far more interesting to engage students in moral quandaries that require them to wrestle with issues they may not have considered before, such as the right to die.

In a democracy, the law should be, as Jefferson suggested, a codification of public opinion. When changes in the moral consensus concerning issues like abortion and capital punishment lead to changes in the law about these issues, it is important for students of the "sociology of law" to examine how this process occurred. But what happens when the moral consensus is unclear about potential moral quandaries that have been created suddenly by new medical technologies? Consider the case of Nancy Cruzan:

The Right to Die

Nancy Cruzan was in a car accident that caused her to be denied oxygen for fourteen minutes. Paramedics revived her but her brain deteriorated to what doctors called a "persistent vegetative state" from which there could be no recovery. Her "cerebral cortical atrophy" was irreversible and permanent. For the next seven years she was kept alive by a feeding and hydration tube and doctors believed that she could be experiencing pain and could "live" another thirty years. Her parents asked the hospital to let her die.

When the hospital refused, the family went to court. The case arrived at the U.S. Supreme Court in 1990. The question presented to the Court was this: Does the Cruzan family have a right under the Constitution to withdraw the feeding tube or may the state of Missouri prohibit them from doing so?

Students ponder this case. There are always some thoughtful questions asked before they begin to suggest their own views. Can we starve our children to death? Will modern medical technology wind up keeping us all "alive" indefinitely? How many others are in a "persistent vegetative state?" How many will be in such a state in the future? Following this initial discussion, students overwhelmingly agree with the position of the Cruzan family. The state of Missouri, they argue, has no right to prevent them from allowing their daughter to die with dignity. However, there is a video of Nancy Cruzan lying in her hospital bed with her eyes open and a doll under her arm. Occasionally, she blinks. Before viewing this video, perhaps eight or nine out of ten students have expressed the opinion that it would be morally acceptable to allow her to starve to death. Once they see her, however, with her eyes open, many seem to blanch. (In fact, on one occasion a student turned ashen and had to leave the room.)

Should the law allow anyone to remove her feeding tube and kill her? Is this death with dignity or criminal homicide? The Cruzan case presented a situation that is becoming more and more common. Medical technology is progressing at such a pace that the law has no precedent to look to for guidance. Nancy Cruzan would have died if her accident had happened in the sixties. Today's miracle technology kept her respiratory and circulatory systems functioning. After many years, her parents could no longer sit back and allow her to go on like this and they argued that the state did not have the right to force them to do so. Interestingly, Solicitor General Kenneth Starr would file an *amicus curiae*, or friend of the court, brief arguing the case against the Cruzans.

Even after seeing the video, a majority of students side with the Cruzan family. If there is no medical hope for improvement and no human life other than a "persistent vegetative state," then justice demands that they be allowed to withdraw the feeding and hydration tube. Students seem reassured that the Court's decision allowed this result. The Court ruled that if the Cruzans could prove to a trial court by "clear and convincing evidence" that Nancy had expressed the view that she would want them to withdraw the tube under these circumstances, then the state of Missouri could not prevent them from doing so. Nancy died shortly after the tube was withdrawn.

In college classrooms of an earlier generation, students would never have considered Nancy's situation. Back then Nancy would have died on the night of her accident. Earlier generations never had to consider what the law should be concerning medical situations created by the miraculous medical technology we take for granted today. The need for a law governing the practice of heart transplants, for instance, or the distinction between heart death and brain death was something we did not worry about. Today's students were born into a world where heart transplants were already common and in class discussion they seem more accepting of rethinking legal doctrines that relate to medical technology. Consider, for instance, the problem of frozen embryos:

The Frozen Heirs

A couple named Lopez was unable to conceive a child through natural methods and decided on *in vitro* fertilization. They were told that a hospital in Australia was very advanced in this procedure, so they flew to Sydney from their home in Los Angeles. He donated some sperm and she had three eggs removed. They were joined in a petri dish and after six weeks the embryos were frozen. The procedure called for Mrs. Lopez to have one of the embryos implanted while the other two would serve as backups.

She never made it back. Mr. and Mrs. Lopez flew their Beechcraft plane out of Los Angeles airport and crashed it into the Pacific Ocean. They died leaving an estate estimated to be worth over $5 million and no living relatives. Or were there "living relatives"?

From a freezer in a lab in a hospital in Sydney, Australia, came three tiny voices. Actually, the voices were represented by the legal department of the hospital, arguing in a California court that the Lopez "children" were the natural descendants of the deceased and that clearly the Lopezes themselves would have wanted the money to be used on their "children." Unpersuaded, the comptroller of California argued that there were no living relatives and therefore the money should revert to the state of California.

What does justice demand in such a situation? Suppose the Lopezes had left a will providing for the hiring of surrogate mothers in the event of their untimely deaths? Would that be a pivotal issue in this case? What if, before their deaths, they had signed contracts providing for surrogate mothers? In that case, should the embryos be considered "direct third-party beneficiaries" of that contract with the power to enforce them? It is a virtual certainty that such a contract would be enforceable by the surrogates themselves. Should a court consider what the Lopezes' preference would be in the current situation?

Is there public consensus about the rights of the embryos and the rights of the state of California in this case? Should the embryos be thawed and destroyed, even though Mr. and Mrs. Lopez intended to carry at least one of them to term and give it life? If we do recognize the right of the Lopez estate to hire a surrogate mother, do all three embryos have an equal claim to the estate? Or just the one that would have been chosen?

Clearly, we need to change the laws that were written before we had the technology to create these situations. Today's students, far more accustomed to abortion on demand than their parents were at their age, are less disturbed at the prospect of throwing away the frozen embryos. However, they are also more concerned about the protection of private property rights, especially when the other party claiming the accumulated savings of Mr. and Mrs. Lopez is the state tax collector.

The result is an argument that seems to be a curious admixture of indifference toward the "rights" of the embryo but a respect for the intent of the Lopezes on how best to dispose of their assets. The right of the state of California does not figure prominently in their reasoning.

How much help can we find in the common law for cases like these? Could the framers of the Constitution have anticipated this kind of problem? Does the embryo deserve to be considered a "person" under the Fourteenth Amendment due process clause when it comes to inheritance rights? Did *Roe v. Wade* resolve this issue? If so, when does that designation begin?

What about frozen embryos involved in property settlements during a divorce? When all of the property is divided between the divorcing couple, should a judge award possession of frozen embryos to one of the parties? This is not a hypothetical question.

"You Keep the SUV but Give Me the Embryos"

A Bakersfield, California, couple had seven embryos frozen for *in vitro* fertilization. Things started going badly for them and they wound up filing for divorce. As part of the settlement, she asked for the seven embryos, indicating that she planned to carry at least one of them to term. The husband argued that he did not want to be forced by the court into fatherhood and that the embryos should be destroyed. What is the just thing to do?

To heighten interest in the case, assume that this might well be the woman's final opportunity to ever become a mother and that if the judge orders these embryos thawed out and flushed away, she will probably never know the joys of motherhood. Students rarely argue that there should be a legal right in the embryos themselves, which the court should acknowledge. For most of them, *Roe v. Wade* settled that issue, though there is always a minority argument that all seven embryos should be saved.

The issue, as most of them see it, is between the conflicting claims of the couple. Should the husband be forced against his will to become a father? Is it too late for him to make that claim? Should the child (or children) wind up on welfare, will he be legally responsible for their support? Should this be treated as a custody battle in which the best interest of the embryos are the paramount concern?

The majority of students generally concur with the decision of the judge in California who ruled in favor of the husband and had the embryos destroyed. However the debate leaves a residual uncertainty about how these cases should be treated in the future and this conversation can be taken a little further. Suppose, for instance, that the embryos had already been implanted in the woman. Does the simple event of implantation suddenly entitle them to legal protection against the father's claim? When does it become the right of the fetus rather than the right of the parents? If a pregnant woman dies, does her fetus have any rights? Again, this is not some theoretical inquiry:

Mom Died and Baby's Still Inside

In San Rafael, California, a woman developed cancer while pregnant. Her boyfriend realized that the tumor in her brain would eventually kill her, but he hoped that she would live long enough to deliver his child. Her mother had a different view. With six weeks left in her pregnancy, the woman succumbed to the tumor. The mother asked the hospital to remove her from the machines that kept her heart beating so that she might bury her daughter. The boyfriend insisted that the "baby" be kept alive in her womb for the next six weeks, at which time the obstetrician could deliver the baby.

The court heard arguments that the mother had a legal right to bury her daughter with dignity and remove her corpse from these hideous machines. They also heard arguments that the natural father—the boyfriend—had the right to bring his child into the world. And, finally, they heard arguments that the fetus had the legal right to remain inside its mother's womb for the next six weeks.

For the first eight centuries of the common law, no one had to answer legal questions like this. Medical technology was such that the fetus died with its mother and both were buried, as the grandmother wished. But rapid advancements in medical technology demand new thinking and, hopefully, this thinking will continue to be based on traditional moral concepts. Does a viable fetus whose chance of survival is greater within its mother's womb have the legal right to prevent its mother's burial? Whose rights take precedence—those of the natural father or those of the grandmother? Would his marital status be relevant to that question?

Here, the overwhelming majority of students side with the position of the father. Even when presented with a hypothetical case in which the fetus is younger, say five months old, most students still insist that the machines should be kept on. Again, they seem to locate the right not in the fetus, but in the mother, father, and the grandmother. Does the father have a superior claim to determine the outcome here over the claim of the woman's mother? As medical technology evolves in ways that were once considered science fiction, the new generation is going to have to wrestle with the moral and legal implications of the questions this technology presents.

In the same way, as the relationship between the sexes continues to change, many laws dealing with that relationship will need to be scrutinized. Consider, for instance, the recent transformation of the law covering the crime of rape.

THE LAW OF RAPE

Some legal changes are demanded not from new technology but from social changes in the way we view long-standing problems. For instance, in virtually every state penal code there have been dramatic changes in the past twenty years in the law governing the crime of rape. It is safe to say that the law concerning no other crime has undergone as much change as that of rape. Much of this has been attributable to the political efforts of various feminist organizations in pressing state legislatures for reform of their penal codes, and most of that reform was long overdue.

Traditionally, rape was treated in the common law as the "forcible unlawful carnal knowledge" of a woman. The term *unlawful* meant that the couple was not legally married. If they were, the act was not unlawful and his assault upon her was not rape. In short, a man could not be convicted of rape for forcing his wife to have intercourse. Over the last two decades numerous states have changed their laws to criminalize marital rape, although a majority of states still do not. Feminist organizations have advocated the reform of penal codes to include marital rape but, at this point, only a minority of states have yet adopted such statutes.

However, in numerous other areas of rape law virtually every state has amended the penal code to modernize the law. For example, there was a time when the felony of rape could not be proven in most state criminal courts unless the testimony of the victim was corroborated by some other piece of evidence. In other words, while a victim could win a conviction in a case of aggravated assault based solely on her uncorroborated word, in a rape trial there had to be some corroboration. Some other piece of evidence had to connect the defendant with the victim or the event in question.

It is not entirely clear why this distinction was made. Why did penal codes make this rather arbitrary distinction between rape law and assault law? Why does the corroboration requirement apply solely to rape? It is worth noting to today's students that rape would always involve a female victim and a male defendant, and males, for the most part, have written the penal codes. It certainly is suggestive of the "standpoint epistemology" about which we spoke in the last chapter. It is very clear that the last few generations were far more inclined to accept this as the natural order of things than the students of today. Perhaps more than any other difference between the students of earlier generations and the students of today is that today's students have a very different view of the relationship between the sexes.

Another example of this is the "Hale Warning," introduced by seventeenth-century English jurist Sir Matthew Hale. In addition to the requirement of corroboration, in most states judges were required to read the Hale Warning to the jury at the end of a rape trial. The Hale Warning states, "Rape is easy to charge and difficult to disprove." Until recently, these were the last words the jury would hear before being sent off to deliberate the guilt or innocence of a defendant charged with rape. During the last quarter century, however, one state after another has questioned the reason for giving such a warning about rape but not about any other crime. Virtually all have changed the law and eliminated the Hale Warning. Today's students are dumbfounded that it took so long to eliminate this palpably sexist tradition.

Yet another change in rape law came in the area of the victim's sexual history. "Shield laws" have been passed in almost every state in the recent past. These laws take different forms but basically they all exclude the sexual history of a rape victim from the trial of the suspected rapist.

The debate over these laws has often been heated and prolonged in various state legislatures.

The demand for reform came in the seventies when numerous examples of abuse came to public attention. Women were being tacitly discouraged from ever reporting a rape by the spectacle of a humiliating cross-examination during the trial. Specifically, after undergoing direct examination by the prosecutor, the victim would then have her character attacked on cross-examination by the defense attorney. Each and every aspect of the woman's sexual history would be laboriously examined in detail as a packed courtroom listened intently. The victims frequently referred to this demeaning ordeal as "the second rape." Women's groups demanded that state legislatures change the law to make any evidence of the victim's past sexual history inadmissible on the grounds that it was irrelevant.

Not everyone agreed with this position. A debate erupted in one state legislature after another between those supporting and those opposing the creation of "shield laws"—laws that would shield the victim from such cross-examination. How could anyone disagree that this humiliating cross-examination was unfair? The usual hypothetical raised by defenders of the existing law went something like this:

The Unfounded Allegation

Danny Defendant is an eighteen-year-old Marine who agreed to pay $50 to have sex with a prostitute. After he paid her they had intercourse but she demanded an additional $50; if he didn't pay, she would call the police. He refused. She had him arrested. He is now being tried for rape. The only issue for the jury is whether or not she consented.

The jury hears her story and she is very convincing, dressed demurely and appearing very much like a "church lady," as presented by the prosecutor. The only possible method of impeaching her credibility is to be able to introduce evidence of her lengthy career in prostitution. Is it fair to eliminate this avenue of cross-examination?

Students grow as emotional in discussing this issue as the legislators did when debating the proposed changes in the Evidence Codes of the various states. Males tend to sympathize with the Marine; females lean heavily toward the rights of the victim. The debate generates a good deal of heat.

The sexual behavior of today's students may be somewhat different from that of their parents' generation, but their attitudes toward the sexual behavior of others is substantially different from those of their parents' generation. This is a generation that is far more tolerant or indifferent toward what others are doing. Homosexuality, for example, is clearly more accepted today than it was in the sixties; at the same time, the so-called "double-standard" is far less accepted.

While sexual promiscuity among males in the sixties was widely tolerated, if not admired, today it is viewed with more suspicion. Female promiscuity, however, seems to have moved in the opposite direction. Generally denounced in the sixties, today's students see it, in some instances, as a kind of political statement and in most cases view it as no one's business but the woman's own. Prince Charles's extramarital adultery makes him, in the eyes of many contemporary students, a cad. The affairs that Princess Diana reportedly engaged in before her death are seen more as a statement of liberation for all women. If a woman, like the hypothetical prostitute/rape victim, has chosen to have sex for money, today's college students are far less judgmental than past generations would have been.

That said, does justice give the young Marine the legal right to introduce the sexual history of the victim in his rape trial? The debate evolves among students and it can be difficult to keep it civil. This particular discussion frequently generates more heat than most other debates. Students sometimes need to be reminded that genuine anger is not inappropriate; but a Jerry Springer–type brawl is. We can agree to disagree but only if we can do it in a rational, informed, and respectful manner. Shouting at each other never moves a discussion toward shared understandings.

Quite often this discussion winds up proposing the actual compromise that most state legislatures arrived at when the shield laws were enacted. Simply stated, the compromise provides that the sexual history of the victim in a rape trial will be presumed to be irrelevant and inadmissible. However, the defense counsel can request a hearing in chambers with the trial court judge to discuss the sexual history of the victim. If defense counsel is able to demonstrate to the trial judge that in this particular case the victim has had a truly "unusual sexual history" and that the exclusion of this evidence would be unfair, the judge can allow the evidence in. So, while the vast majority of victims will have their sexual history excluded from trial, the young Marine in this case will clearly be allowed to explain the sexual history of the prostitute. For the time being, at least, this is as close to "justice" as we can get.

CONCLUSION

We began this chapter with the Latin maxim of law, *Cessante ratione legis, cessat ipsa lex.* We have seen in this chapter how often the "reason for the law" can cease to exist, as in sexist rape laws, in laws regarding people caught in a "persistent vegetative state," or in the law regarding frozen embryos. The framers of the Constitution in 1787 could have anticipated none of these challenges to our legal tradition. However, the framers did have enough insight to understand that changing times would bring about a need for changing the fundamental law of the land. With that in mind, they provided for an amendment process to their great masterpiece, the longest-lasting constitution in the history of our species. We will look at the U.S. Constitution in Chapter 4.

SUGGESTED READINGS

Posner, R. (1996). *The federal courts: The challenge and reform.* Cambridge, MA: Harvard University Press.

Taslitz, R.E. (1999). *Rape and the culture of the courtroom.* New York: New York University Press.

Watson, A. (1997). *Sources of law, legal change and ambiguity.* Philadelphia: University of Pennsylvania Press.

Zitrin, R.A. & Zangford, C. (1999). *The moral compass of the American lawyer: Truth, justice, power and greed.* New York: Ballantine Books.

Chapter 4

The Constitution

Is it really anything the court says it is? If the "tyranny of the ma-jority" can only be prevented by a "committee of unelected law-yers" through the power of "judicial review," have we substituted one form of tyranny for another and effectively de-stroyed democratic rule?

The Constitution of the United States enjoys a fascinating devotion among the American public, including today's college students. How-ever, the ultimate arbiter of what that document means is, of course, the U.S. Supreme Court, and the image of that august body has not fared nearly as well with either group. In short, students seem to continue to show the same reverence for the Constitution that their parents feel but at the same time they are far more likely to question the legitimacy of the nine people who interpret it.

This is in no small measure attributable to the campaign that began in some political circles during the era of the Warren Court and is con-tinued today by scholars like Robert Bork, Ronald Reagan's failed nominee to the Court. Bork and his supporters in academe argue that the Court is "antidemocratic." He maintains that the Justices are simply "a committee of unelected lawyers" and that the whole idea of "judicial review" is antidemocratic and wrong. Moreover, Bork has argued that judicial review was wrong in 1803 when Chief Justice John Marshall enunciated the principle in the case of *Marbury v. Madison*. (Judicial review empowers the Court to strike down any law that the Justices believe violates the Constitution.)

"Why," Bork asks, "should five out of nine Justices be empowered to overthrow a law passed, perhaps unanimously, by the democratically elected members of the other two branches of government?" What if all 535 members of the Senate and the House of Representatives vote for an enormously popular bill that is then signed into law by the president. Why should five unelected Justices on the other side of town be allowed to strike down such a law? A very large majority of today's students concur with Bork that such an outcome is antidemocratic. The challenge is to see if they have considered the other perspective.

THE U.S. CONSTITUTION

This discussion has to start with some basics about our fundamental law. The U.S. Constitution has been in effect for over two centuries and that makes it the oldest constitution in human history. It has also been the template for dozens of emerging nations trying to create their own fundamental law, including some of the newly emancipated communist-bloc nations. The worldwide influence of the U.S. Constitution on other nations of the Earth makes it fair to suggest that the Constitution of our founding fathers is the most important constitution ever written.

It is also fair to suggest that there is no nation in which a constitution plays as important a role as the United States. The reason for this has to do with our cultural heterogeneity. Of the 200 or so nation-states on the planet, there is none that is more culturally diverse than the United States. The importance of this diversity—referred to by anthropologists as "cultural heterogeneity"—is difficult to overstate. Nation-states that enjoy a substantial homogeneity in their culture are not as dependent on a constitution—or, for that matter, on a legal system in general—as nations that are diverse. Like families that are not terribly dysfunctional, homogeneous nations do not need a lot of lawyers to resolve their differences. They simply understand that they have the same values, feel the same fears and pains, and share a sense of "togetherness." Consider the ties that bind together the people of homogeneous nations.

The Japanese are the Japanese, with or without the constitution that we lent them after the war. They share one language, just two major religions, the same food and traditions and culture. The English are the English—about 95 percent white, Anglo-Saxon members of the Anglican Church who speak the same language, celebrate the same holidays, and share the same history and religion and ancestors. The French people are virtually all the descendants of the same ancient tribes that trod the fields of Gaul 2,000 years ago. The French actually went through five constitutions following the war but they always remained "the French." Their constitution could make them a fascist republic, or a Christian democracy, or a communist dictatorship or even a monarchy. But they would still have that feeling of "togetherness" that grows out of cultural homogeneity. How does this compare to the United States of America?

Americans are descended from virtually every tribe that ever existed. We come from countless races, religions, and ethnic groups, with all the differences that can be imagined. While three out of four Americans are non-Hispanic whites, even this "majority" group has enormous ethnic diversity. Virtually every European nation is represented in that group and in most cases their ancestors could not even communicate with one another.

We celebrate Christmas, but we also celebrate Chanukah and Kwaanza and Ramadan. There are over 100 languages spoken in both New York City and Los Angeles. The World Almanac lists over 150 different religious groups in the United States with more than 10,000 members. (The Baptists have 15 different churches. Islam is tenth largest with 3.3 million; Hindus have over 1 million American members.) With religious diversity like that, there is little doubt as to why Americans view their Constitution with an almost spiritual reverence. Other than the World Series and the Super Bowl, it is just about the only thing that holds all of us together.

For over 210 years, Americans have functioned under one Constitution, with just seventeen Amendments following the Bill of Rights. No nation in history has ever owed so much to a document. To put that in perspective, the Soviet Union went through seven constitutions in the seven decades it existed before collapsing.

Political scientists have argued that the reason the U.S. Constitution has lasted so long is because its framers had the foresight to build into it both stability and flexibility. In other words, it created legal relationships that were difficult to change, so that Americans could resist the fleeting passions of the day when the polls would show a majority willing to scrap some fundamental right. But, at the same time, when social needs really did require a change in our fundamental law, the amendment process, while slow and cumbersome, was nonetheless ultimately available.

TODAY'S STUDENTS' VIEW OF THE CONSTITUTION

Today's students still perceive the enormous reverence that the nation in general feels for the U.S. Constitution, and they express it in class. In a time of transformative social changes, the Constitution embodies a permanence that these students find reassuring. Change may be pervasive in marriages and families and jobs and the economy but the fundamental freedoms guaranteed by this document remain. The one thing that holds Americans together is the set of ideas expressed in the U.S. Constitution, summarized most succinctly by the four words on the tympanum of the Supreme Court building: "Equal Justice Under Law." Almost without exception, the students agree with that proposition.

At the same time, many of today's students are aware of a debate among political scientists concerning the Supreme Court's role in the proper interpretation of the Constitution. Does the power of "judicial review" eliminate democratic rule? Does it give tyrannical power to the Supreme Court to ban the right to say a prayer in a public school but guarantee the right to kill a fetus or burn the American flag? Today's students feel very strongly about this issue.

In his classic book *Democracy in America*, Alexis de Tocqueville observed that "scarcely any political question that arises in the United States is not resolved, sooner or later, into a judicial question." In other words, sooner or later, all important political questions arrive at the Supreme Court. No other court in the world has the power of judicial review. Courts elsewhere can interpret the meaning of the legislature in passing a law, but they cannot say that the legislature did not have the right to pass such a law—that the law itself is "unconstitutional" and therefore null and void. It is only in American jurisprudence that such a power exists—and it is an enormous power from the perspective of the political system.

Those who disagree with the argument that Robert Bork raises worry that the legitimacy of, and public confidence in, the Supreme Court will be undermined if the people believe that the Justices are simply engaged in purely personal political judgments. In essence, Bork calls for finding the "original intent" of the framers by adhering to a "strict construction" of the Constitution. If it is not mentioned in the original document, than it should not be interpreted as being there. By and large, our students believe that he is right.

THE OTHER SIDE OF THE STORY

A cynic once claimed that "The Constitution means whatever the Supreme Court says it means." In other words, it is a blatantly political document that can be twisted to accommodate any imaginable concept. While there is very little in American constitutional history that would justify this cynicism, there certainly is some truth in the observation that the members of the Supreme Court "read the newspapers." In other words, the interpretation of the meaning of the provisions in the Constitution is necessarily influenced by the social, economic, and political realities of the day. The Constitution's "convenient vagueness" has enabled it to survive as well as it has.

There are numerous terms in the Constitution that allow for wide-ranging interpretation. In different eras of Court history, various interpretations have been given to terms like *due process, cruel and unusual punishment, equal protection,* and *unreasonable searches.* The proper interpretation of much of the Constitution has undergone some interesting changes over the last few decades and this situation becomes quickly apparent to professors educated in the sixties and teaching today's generation of college students. Consider the student reaction to two controversial cases from the Supreme Court, one in 1962 and the other in 1989.

Prayer in Public Schools

Sometime in the fifties, the New York State Board of Regents composed a short prayer for all public school children to recite before class began. A group of ten parents—led by Steven Engel—brought a suit claiming that prayer in the public school violated the establishment clause of the First Amendment. The prayer was both short and nonsectarian but it had been written by a state official and had to be read in every class. In *Engel v. Vitale* (1962) the Court ruled in favor of Engel and, in effect, banned prayer in the public schools in the future.

At the time of the school prayer decision, the public's reaction was muted by today's standards. The polls at the time indicated that the public did not agree with the decision but there was hardly anything that could be called a public outrage. However, like all unpopular decisions, this case drained a significant amount of the public's reservoir of good will for the Court. Political conservatives have used the school prayer decision for almost four decades to exemplify the arrogance of their opponents on the left and the "judicial activism" of the Supreme Court.

Like *Roe v. Wade* and some of the early affirmative action cases, the school prayer case simply alienated a large part of the public. Decisions that are this unpopular could probably never have been reached by an elected legislature. Elected officials, unlike Supreme Court Justices, keep their eye on public opinion polls much too closely to ever vote in favor of something as unpopular as the removal of prayer from public schools. Consider, for instance, the Supreme Court decision in *Johnson v. Texas* (1989):

Flag Burning

Gregory Johnson was very angry with the United States, especially the Republican party. In order to express his anger he bought an American flag, took it to a public site outside the 1984 Republican National Convention in Dallas and burned it. He was arrested and convicted under a Texas statute that made it a crime to engage in "the desecration of a venerated object."

The U.S. Supreme Court ruled that the First Amendment protected Johnson's right to engage in this form of protest. Polls showed that an overwhelming majority of Americans disagreed with this decision and a U.S. Senate Resolution condemning it passed by a vote of 97 to 3. A comparable House of Representatives Resolution passed 411–15. The Flag Protection Act of 1989 sought to reinstate punishment for flag burning, but in 1990 the Court again struck down the law as violating the First Amendment and "diluting the very freedom that makes this emblem so revered and worth revering."

Students regularly jump out of their seats about this case. By more than three to one, college students oppose this decision and argue that flag burning should be a punishable offense. Far more disturbing, however, is that students also question the very authority of the Court to impose its will on the majority of voters.

If the overwhelming majority of American voters want the law to punish an activity, how can a democratic system prevent the majority from ruling? Madison and Hamilton voiced a considerable amount of worry about the "tyranny of the majority," which they foresaw in the new democracy. In the Federalist Papers, they conjured up the possibility of 51 percent of the voters imposing its will—without restriction—upon their fellow Americans.

Assume, for example, that the polls indicate that a majority of Americans—perhaps an overwhelming majority—are fearful about the role of a small group. Let us assume that a group of "blue-eyed, Lutheran Eskimos" gets a good deal of negative press and a growing number of editorials demand their expulsion from public education everywhere. If polls show that 85 percent of Americans would approve of such a discriminatory law, surely at least one of the 535 members of Congress would introduce the "blue-eyed Lutheran Eskimo exclusion act" in hopes of getting favorable media coverage.

What if such a bill were to become a law? Say, the House of Representatives votes overwhelmingly for it; the Senate passes it by a resounding vote; the president—with a keen eye on the polls—signs it into law. The next day, all students in public schools who are "blue-eyed Lutheran Eskimos" are expelled from school. This is "the tyranny of the majority" about which Madison and Hamilton were concerned.

How can a democracy shield itself from the popular will of the voters when the rights of some people are being blatantly violated? Should the majority rule no matter what? Students need to keep in mind the distinction between a "majoritarian state" and a "constitutional democracy." A pure democracy is a majoritarian state; that is, the majority always prevails without regard to individual rights. In a constitutional democracy, the will of the majority can be thwarted by the constitutional rights of an individual. But who can enforce these rights?

If the legislative and the executive branches are both subject to periodic elections, they are inclined to follow the will of the majority of voters, regardless of how much that policy might trample on the rights of the minority. The way we avoid this "tyranny of the majority" is by creating a Supreme Court with the power of "judicial review." It works like this: Popularly elected legislators in the South passed laws that prohibited African-Americans from attending school with whites. It is unlikely that these officials would ever have voted to repeal these segregation laws if they were left to their own political instincts.

A Kansas statute, for instance, authorized local school boards to "maintain separate schools for the education of white and colored students." However, in 1954 when the nine Justices of the Supreme Court heard the arguments on behalf of a young African-American school girl named Linda Brown, they ruled in *Brown v. the Board of Education of Topeka, Kansas,* that such laws violated the equal protection clause of the Fourteenth Amendment. Accordingly, these laws were declared unconstitutional and therefore null and void. Was that decision antidemocratic?

Brown was a very unpopular decision when it was handed down, perhaps the most unpopular decision of the 20th century. If the question presented to the Court in *Brown* had instead awaited the action of a democratically elected legislature, the law would probably still today guarantee racial segregation in many of our public schools.

It is also very unlikely that popularly elected governors and legislatures would have extended the constitutional rights of criminal suspects as they were extended by the Court during the 1960s. Certainly, the First Amendment right to be free from compulsory prayer in public schools or to protest U.S. political policy by burning an American flag may never enjoy the support of a majority of voters. Should the majority be entitled to impose its view on others in these areas? Are there other options available to the voters?

The flag-burning case was so unpopular with the American public that polls were showing as many as 90 percent of respondents suggesting that the Court was wrong. Political leaders naturally jumped on the bandwagon and denounced the High Court ruling with all the righteous indignation of anyone facing upcoming elections. Certainly, the public image of the Court was not helped by its exercise of the power of judicial review in the flag burning case. Some observers went as far as to question the value of judicial review itself.

It should be noted in this context that jurisprudential scholars who believe that judicial review is undemocratic also believe that it should be abolished. They generally argue that the judicial activism of the 1960s and 1970s caused the Court to abandon the "original intent" of the framers of the Constitution and ignore the traditional, "strict construction" of the clauses of the Constitution. The Justices then wind up acting as an unelected "super legislature" that initiates new directions on public policy issues. In the words of Robert Bork, what we were watching was "a limited coup d'état by a committee of nine unelected lawyers."

The charge that the power of judicial review is antidemocratic—because it involves a small number of unelected judges reversing the will of the democratically elected representatives—has historically been made more often by those who happen to disagree with the decisions being handed down by the Court. For instance, toward the end of his second term, Ronald Reagan nominated Robert Bork as a Justice of the

Supreme Court. Bork was questioned by the Senate Judiciary Committee about his judicial philosophy and, more specifically, about how he felt about the Court decision in *Griswold v. Connecticut*. Bork stated that he would have joined the sole dissenter in *Griswold*, Potter Stewart. Consider the facts of that case:

Criminalizing Condoms?

In 1961, Estelle Griswold provided birth control information to three married women in Connecticut. She was arrested, prosecuted, and convicted under a statute that made it a crime to use, or aid and abet in the use of, contraceptives and provided a punishment of a year in jail for its violation. This was a nineteenth-century statute, which had been unsuccessfully challenged in the Connecticut legislature twenty-nine times during the four decades preceding Griswold's arrest. The elected officials of Connecticut had refused to repeal or modify the anticontraceptive law.

In 1965, the U.S. Supreme Court ruled that the Constitution provides a certain right to privacy—especially in the marital relationship—which the state may not violate. While the right to use contraceptives is not specified anywhere in the Constitution, a "penumbra" is created by various sections of the Constitution, which cannot be denied or disparaged simply because it is not enumerated. Griswold's conviction was reversed.

Students today are so shocked by the facts of the Griswold case that they often think that they must have heard the facts incorrectly. They find it very hard to believe that any government anywhere would have ever claimed the right to incarcerate someone for *using* a condom. In their minds, *not* using a condom might be something that should be criminalized, but it is inconceivable that the Constitution would not protect an individual who chose to act responsibly.

When Robert Bork was asked about the *Griswold* decision during his confirmation hearings, he argued that *Griswold* was incorrectly decided because if the "majority" of Connecticut citizens elect a legislature that prohibits the dispensing of birth control devices, then the Court has no right to overrule the will of the majority by declaring such a prohibition unconstitutional. Others would suggest that a state prohibition on birth control or birth control education would certainly fall into the area of "tyranny of the majority."

Robert Bork has blamed "liberal Justices" for taking an "activist" stance by using judicial review to undo the work of conservative legislatures that were elected by a majority of voters. But David O'Brien points out that while scholars like Bork say the Court is no longer, in Hamilton's words, "the least dangerous branch," the conservative Burger and Rehnquist Courts have been just as activist as the liberal Warren Court—but in the opposite political direction. Consider, for example, *City of Richmond v. Croson* (1989). In that case the Court overturned a law passed by the majority of the Richmond City Council. The law benefited blacks by providing a "setaside program" for the city's minorities who bid on construction contracts. That decision—written by Justice Rehnquist and joined in by the Court's conservatives—thwarted the will of the City Council who were elected by a majority of the voters of Richmond. And this "committee of unelected lawyers" did so through the use of judicial review. So the traditional conservative objections to judicial activism would seem to depend on whose ox is being gored. The recent dramatic decision in the case of *Gore v. Bush* (2000) only emphasizes this point.

While conservative constitutional scholars like David Horowitz and Raoul Berger decry the use of judicial review to overturn the will of an elected legislature, they ignore the fact that judicial review was a key concern of the framers of the Constitution. Moreover, the framers had little use for unrestrained, popular, majoritarian government. In other words, the framers were fearful of the tyranny of the majority and would clearly approve of the restrictions placed on that tyranny by judicial review.

In fact, the call for a federal constitutional convention resulted from a desire to curb this excess of democracy in the states and increasingly, the protection of the rights of a minority—such as property holders and creditors—became a central concern. Therefore, to interpret the Constitution today to require the protection of minority rights over the will of the majority may be, as Alexander Bickel says, "counter-majoritarian," but it is not inconsistent with the framers' intent.

SUGGESTED READINGS

Bork, R. (1990). *The tempting of America: The political seduction of the law.* New York: The Free Press.

Cox, A. (1968). *The Warren court: Constitutional decision as an instrument of reform.* Cambridge, MA: Harvard University Press.

Dewey, J. (1916). *Democracy and education.* New York: The Free Press.

Kaus, M. (1989, November 6). Bork chop. *New Republic,* 118–119.

Schwartz, H. (Ed.). (1987). *The Burger years: Rights and wrongs in the Supreme Court, 1969–1986.* New York: Viking.

Tribe, L.H. (1999). *American constitutional law.* Mineola, NY: Foundation Press.

Chapter 5

The Bill of Rights

How is justice best served by the judicial interpretation of things like the "establishment clause," the "equal protection clause," and the "due process clause?"

There is probably no more respected symbol of American liberty than the Bill of Rights. Cobbled together by the framers after lengthy debate in the sweltering heat of the summer of 1789, the first ten amendments to the Constitution were ratified by the states in 1791. A good indication of the extraordinary stability of the U.S. system of government is that, over the past two centuries, there have only been another seventeen changes in the Constitution ratified, and two of them canceled each other out. (Some very thirsty voters repealed the Prohibition amendment in 1933.)

The Bill of Rights and the Fourteenth Amendment have been involved in far more of the 10,000 cases that the U.S. Supreme Court has heard than all the rest of the Constitution. They have also been at the heart of innumerable political issues that have troubled the nation throughout its history. Most often, the issue involves a dispute between an individual who claims a constitutional right to do something that the government claims the right to prohibit. The opinion of today's college students about the proper resolution of these disputes says a lot about the moral values that these students support most strongly.

In this chapter, we shall consider just three clauses from the Bill of Rights—the *establishment clause* of the First Amendment, the *equal protection* clause and the *due process* clause of the Fourteenth Amendment.

THE ESTABLISHMENT CLAUSE OF THE FIRST AMENDMENT

The very first clause of the First Amendment agreed upon by the framers of the Bill of Rights was not the right to free speech, or press, or assembly, or even the right to freely exercise one's religion. It was the prohibition on the establishment of religion. The history of religious oppression in England was clearly linked to the fervor with which the framers approached this subject. They had already provided for a secular electoral process in the Constitution that had been written two years prior to the Bill of Rights. (Article VI says that "no religious test shall ever be required as a qualification to any office or public trust . . .")

Nonetheless, the very first words of the Bill of Rights forbid Congress from passing any law respecting the "establishment of religion." This line would be interpreted in widely different ways by various political factions 200 years later. In the last chapter we saw how strongly most college students react to the school prayer decision. By and large, today's students think it was a mistake to ban prayer in the public schools. They also believe that government should be more supportive of church activities and many will argue that churches, in general, are more efficient at implementing poverty programs than the government.

They followed the presidential race of 2000 and they saw that virtually all the candidates advocated making the "wall of separation" between church and state somewhat more porous than it is today. As a decade of Court decisions chipped away at the wall, the *New York Times* would suggest that "We're just one or two votes away on the Supreme Court from a radical redefinition of what church-state separation means." In other words, the High Court appears to be on the verge of replacing the strict separation principle with something very different. For the most part, students consider this a good idea. They do not understand the underlying rationale for "separation of church and state" and seem inadequately informed about its history.

Thomas Jefferson had talked about a "wall of separation" between the church and the state, and, in his day, it was probably true that the state could have been controlled by the church. Theocracies were still the norm in the late 18th century, and the church played a major role in the lives of most Americans. Today, it seems overwhelmingly clear that the roles of churches and states have been reversed.

There are a growing number of elected officials who are calling for increased government reliance on the social welfare activities of churches and religious charities. Both Republican and Democratic presidential candidates spoke enthusiastically about their support for expanding "faith-based" government spending.

A U.S. Supreme Court decision in June 2000 held that officially sanctioned prayer presented at a public high school football game violated the establishment clause. This appeared to strengthen the wall of separation and suggests that, except for the private prayers said by students facing final exams, American schools would not soon be the site of prayers. However, a week later the Court handed down a much more far-reaching decision dealing with public support of religious schools. A Louisiana school district provided tax dollars for school computers. About 30 percent of the funds went to religious schools and the law authorizing these funds was challenged under the establishment clause. In a surprising decision that suggests future support for such funding, the High Court approved the school district's practice.

More importantly, several cases involving school vouchers for religious schools are working their way toward the Supreme Court. The Louisiana decision implies that such voucher schemes may well be approved and public funding of religious schools could well be in the nation's future.

School vouchers appear to enjoy widespread political support—including that of most college students. With a Supreme Court sympathetic toward modifying the wall of separation and political candidates expressing support for faith-based social services, it is not unrealistic to expect an increasingly privatized public sphere in the coming years, with education and welfare services contracted out to religious organizations on a wide scale. There is so little opposition among students to this erosion of the wall of separation that it is worthwhile playing devil's advocate and presenting the possible downside to all this.

A professor on sabbatical leave walked into a Russian Orthodox Church in Leningrad in 1978. There were no pews, so he stood in the crowd and observed the three priests who were partially concealed by two giant wrought-iron gates at the front of the altar. Women in babushkas continually walked around the church bowing in front of statues of saints called icons. While it was a different kind of religious experience for him, it also gave rise to a curiously disturbing feeling. This "church" did not feel like the churches he had experienced in the United States. Clearly, this was a church that was allowed to open only when the state said that it could. It is unlikely that anything in the sermon could be critical of the Soviet government. Here was a group of priests who were probably supported by the state during their working years and pensioned off after retirement. In other words, this was an unabashedly state-dominated church—something he felt should never happen in a free society.

In recent decades, there has been a political push for more state support for churches in the United States. While these efforts appear to be aimed merely at bolstering churches rather than imposing government control of religion, the professor's memory of Leningrad was haunting. Why would American clerics push for more involvement of the state with their churches? Where was it all heading?

A few years after that trip, the professor's daughter was attending Georgetown University. All the parents of undergraduates received a letter from the Jesuit priest who served as the president of the university. The letter explained that although Catholic doctrine taught that homosexual behavior was sinful, Georgetown was required to begin providing facilities for the Gay Students Association. The letter pointed out that since Georgetown accepted federal money, the law required that they not discriminate against people based on their sexual orientation.

The following year one of the professor's colleagues took her son to college for his freshman year. The university had been a "Catholic university" when her brother graduated from there decades ago. Now, however, because it accepted government money, it could only call itself a university "in the Catholic tradition" and had to teach all religions, not just Catholicism. The state, it seemed, was becoming the camel in the tent. Would "federal guidelines" that accompany federal dollars soon turn American churches into that Leningrad mass? Can churches that accept government funding expect to retain their autonomy? Will government funding of church-run programs turn our churches into quasi–social service providers?

There are current proposals for tax dollars funding massive "faith-based" social service programs. Will the churches be swamped with lawyers and accountants and federal bureaucrats looking over their shoulders to make sure they are using the funds for secular purposes? If this happens, will they still be churches at all?

A Tax-Sponsored Nativity Scene

The small town of Pawtucket, Rhode Island, had celebrated Christmas by setting up a municipally owned nativity scene in a private park (*Lynch v. Donnelly,* 1984). The cost of the display could not have been much, but it was paid for with tax dollars. A taxpayer brought a lawsuit against this practice, arguing that it violated the establishment clause of the First Amendment. The U.S. Supreme Court granted certiorari, meaning it agreed to hear the case.

It seemed clear that the statues of Jesus, Mary, and Joseph were clearly religious figures and that spending tax dollars on this display was helping to "establish" a religion. But the Court disagreed. While there appears to be a good deal of confusion among the Justices about this issue, they seem to be suggesting that government may not "endorse" religion, but the government may "recognize" religion.

For the most part, students feel this case was decided correctly. They believe that government today demonstrates an unseemly hostility toward religion and they do not understand why. They ask what harm could possibly arise out of tax dollars being used to pay for a nativity scene in a city hall.

Cases following *Lynch v. Donnelly* have established the idea that publicly sponsored religious displays are permissible only if they are "secularized." So a Christmas tree is a secular symbol of the Christmas season and may be publicly funded. Moreover, if there is enough of a secular flavor to the display, then religious symbols may also be included. Does this convoluted reasoning open the door for state domination of religion? Is this the start of a process in which the state may dictate what symbols may and may not be included in Christmas displays? If tax dollars can be used to pay for statues of Jesus, Mary, and Joseph, is it not up to some government bureaucrat—or the elected mayor or city council—to determine where and how they can be displayed and how the "greatest story ever told" will be told in the future?

Perhaps questions will be raised as to why there is no "diversity" in this government-sponsored display? Could we not make one of the wise men a wise woman? Must they all be heterosexual? Why does the story always portray Joseph as the carpenter and Mary as the stay-at-home spouse? Is it not possible that Mary was the primary breadwinner? Are these statues really "secular symbols?" Should public tax dollars be paying for all this?

If a growing number of voters see these changes as beneficial, will they accept the infusion of policy into their religions? How long before we hear the argument that nonrabbis should be employed as inspectors of Kosher foods? The memory of that professor's description of mass in Leningrad is very disturbing. Are we headed in the direction of a state-dominated church? Are we inviting the camel into the tent with the hope that there will still be room for religious freedom a generation from now?

A federal appeals court in Texas has ruled that public schools may have a prayer at their graduation ceremonies but only if school officials review the prayer in advance to make sure there is no reference to Jesus. So, while some may argue that prayer should not be imposed on people who do not want it, the argument could be made that the state has no business censoring the content of that prayer. And while we are discussing religion in Texas, it may be wise to remember that one of the best known of the Texas religious leaders was David Koresh of the Branch Davidians. If there is to be widespread funding for religious groups, certainly groups like the Branch Davidians will have to be given equal treatment by the government.

The vast majority of today's students take out college loans from the government and they are familiar with the nightmare of the bureaucratic forms necessary to secure these loans. So it is not surprising to them that grants from government come with strings attached and that those strings can become very controlling. For the most part, those students who belong to churches recoil at the thought of government interference with the independence of their churches. In short, the "wall of separation" that Jefferson suggested should exist between church and state does not seem to be as bad an idea as they thought.

Americans have always been deeply religious and deeply suspicious of state-imposed uniformity. That suspicion may prove very useful in these changing times. Could the federal government tell a church-affiliated college that by accepting government student loans they may no longer ban homosexual dating on campus, even when such behavior violates the canons of the church? Is Jefferson's wall of separation as bad for religion as some church leaders now argue? Simple answers to these questions are almost always unsatisfying to today's students.

THE FOURTEENTH AMENDMENT

A little history is important to an understanding of the Fourteenth Amendment. After the Civil War, Congress watched in horror as resentful Southern whites came back to their ruined homes and looked angrily at the newly freed slaves. Vengeance was pervasive and ruthless. Everything from lynching to foreclosures and seizure of property were commonplace as "Jim Crow" laws systematically discriminated against the black population of the old Confederacy. Congress sought to "do something."

In 1868 Congress sent the "Civil War amendments" (i.e., the Thirteenth, Fourteenth, and Fifteenth Amendments) to the states for ratification. The thirteenth codified the Emancipation Proclamation and banned involuntary servitude in the United States. The fifteenth extended the right to vote to the newly freed black citizens. But the Fourteenth Amendment was targeted at the fundamental unfairness and the pervasive discrimination practiced by the white establishment.

THE EQUAL PROTECTION CLAUSE

Today's students enjoy debating the morality of a woman in the armed forces who wishes to apply for combat duty. As a career soldier, she realizes that advancement in the military is facilitated by serving in combat units, but the present law prohibits women from serving in such units. Does that prohibition constitute an injustice against women? Does that regulation violate the Constitution? Should it be struck down under the "equal protection clause?" Students debate this issue with some enthusiasm. Female students are more likely to find this discriminatory, but are by no means unanimous in that view. Males, likewise, split on the issue, with a majority sensing that the restriction is reasonable.

The equal protection clause of the Fourteenth Amendment has been at the heart of every civil rights case that the Supreme Court has considered. Indeed, recent cases challenging affirmative action programs as a form of reverse discrimination are also being argued under this clause. While students generally understand and support the intent of the equal protection clause, they also tend to be confused about how this clause is implemented in actual cases. Some fundamentals need to be understood.

Some forms of discrimination are allowable under the Constitution. It is only when that discrimination is arbitrary that it violates the law.

When a waiter in a bar tells a customer who is a gay, African-American, Jewish, female, and in a wheelchair, "We don't serve your kind," can she sue for discrimination? Students invariably say *yes*. They immediately sense that such an action is discriminatory and should be illegal. When asked if everyone agrees that this person's constitutional rights have been violated, they all agree. When asked if their answer would be different if she were sixteen years old, they all get the point. Under some circumstances, it is constitutional to discriminate against people.

Assume that a recruit in the U.S. Navy wants to serve in the Submarine Corps. If the recruit is excluded because of race, religion, or gender, the Constitution has been violated and virtually all students agree that any other outcome would be morally wrong. When students are asked if it would be morally wrong to eliminate a candidate because he is gay, a debate begins. Students today seem far more tolerant of diverse sexual orientation than past generations. However, there are many students—predominantly male—who have serious reservations about serving on a submarine with gay shipmates. The current policy on gays in the military is still unsettled and their generation will have to resolve the issue eventually. However, it is important to understand the point that sometimes discrimination is allowable and debate on the issue can clarify why.

Assume that the recruit is acceptable to the Submarine Corps in every way, but he happens to be six foot, ten inches tall. Is it unfair to eliminate him as a candidate? The students seem to understand that he will not fit into a submarine (unless they pass him in like a torpedo) and that no court is going to force the Navy to modify its ships in order to accommodate him.

So, when can we constitutionally discriminate? The answer is that discrimination is allowable when there is a "rational basis" for making the distinction between this individual and others. The courts refer to this as the "rational basis test" and a distinction that is made without this "rational basis" is called an "invidious classification." Such a classification violates the equal protection clause. With that as a basic introduction, let us consider less obvious cases of discrimination.

Do Statutory Rape Laws Discriminate?

A statutory rape defendant in California was convicted of a felony and sentenced to three years in prison for having consensual intercourse with his girlfriend who was under eighteen years of age. He appealed his conviction to the U.S. Supreme Court under the equal protection clause.

His argument was this: It may be constitutional for the state to punish everyone—male or female—who has sex with a minor, male or female; it certainly would be constitutional to punish no one for having sex with a minor. But it is "an invidious classification" to say that an adult woman may legally have intercourse with a seventeen-year-old male (and perhaps write an article about her affair for *Cosmopolitan* magazine), while a male having intercourse with his seventeen-year-old girlfriend is given three years in prison. The Court's task was to determine whether or not there was a "rational basis" for this distinction.

Students considering this fact pattern initially argue that there is no reason to make this distinction, that the law therefore discriminates against males and the conviction should be reversed. But what is the underlying rationale for statutory rape laws? Why does the legislature put these laws in the penal code in the first place? Should the law prohibit consensual sexual relations involving minors? What is the legislature trying to protect?

Students eventually get around to identifying the government's interest in protecting young women from the consequences of sexual behavior, which they may be too young to understand. Surely, the law should protect an individual of limited understanding from being sexually exploited by an adult. But is there a difference in the potential consequences for young males and young females? Obviously, young males can be victims of sexually transmitted diseases and can be heartbroken by unrequited love. However, young males do not get pregnant and it is this distinction that was the pivotal issue in the Court's decision.

The state's interest in protecting young women is greater than its interest in protecting young men from the dangers of youthful intercourse and that difference forms the "rational basis" that justifies statutory rape laws. Accordingly, the Court ruled in favor of California and upheld the conviction.

By and large, students accept the reasoning of the Court in this case. They can see that female "victims" of statutory rape are more vulnerable than male "victims" and deserve greater protection under the law. But they frequently question the need for governmental protection of anyone beyond their adolescence in their sex lives. They question the fundamental fairness of laws prohibiting any kind of sex between freely consenting adults. This concept of "fundamental fairness" finds constitutional protection in the due process clause.

THE DUE PROCESS OF LAW

The Fifth and Fourteenth Amendments prohibit the government from depriving any person of "life, liberty or property without due process of law." The Fifth refers to the federal government while the Fourteenth applies to the states. The countless attempts by jurists to define the meaning of the term "due process of law" could fill a room. The term itself retains what legal scholars have called "a convenient vagueness"; that is, a flexibility that allows judges in different eras to apply it to changing social conditions. Perhaps the most common definition of due process is the simple definition given it by Justice Felix Frankfurter, who said it meant "fundamental fairness."

In the years following the Civil War, Congress was horrified by the various practices that vengeful white Southerners were using against the newly freed African-Americans. When seeking to pass a single federal law that would prohibit everything from lynching to property seizures to punishments without trial, Congress decided to ordain that "no state shall deny any person life, liberty or property without due process of law." The wording had to be very broad because it was aimed at such a wide variety of behaviors.

The clause has been used by the Court to resolve an enormous number of cases, ranging from school suspensions to imposing the death penalty. In general, conservative Justices give a narrow meaning to the term while liberal Justices tend to define the term broadly. Conservatives frequently complain that the clause has been used by liberal Justices to prohibit anything that their own political views find offensive. A few of these cases can exemplify the point the conservatives are making. Consider *Goss v. Lopez*:

A Lunchroom Disturbance

Dwight Lopez was an Ohio high school student in 1971. A disturbance in his lunchroom resulted in damage to school property and a teacher identified Dwight as being responsible for the disturbance. He was suspended from school for ten days pursuant to an Ohio statute that allowed for such a suspension. His parents retained counsel who sued the school, arguing that the Ohio statute violated Dwight's right to due process of law since it did not provide for any type of hearing in which he could present his side of the case. A three-judge panel in Ohio ruled in favor of Lopez and the high school appealed to the U.S. Supreme Court. Goss was the school's principal.

All four of the Nixon appointees to the Court ruled in favor of the high school. They argued that there was nothing in the meaning of the due process clause that authorized the federal government to tell the school districts of Ohio how to discipline rowdy students. By and large, students reviewing this case concur with the Nixon appointees. Many students who plan to become teachers wonder what their authority will be in their own classrooms. Will a third-grade teacher need to provide a legal aid attorney before making a student stay after school? Will kindergartners be entitled to a jury trial before being denied recess?

How could the Court stretch the meaning of "due process" to cover the Lopez case? Teachers need flexibility to deal appropriately with discipline problems and appellate courts should not be looking over their shoulders every time they need to suspend a student. For that reason, students are frequently dumbfounded when they discover that the four Nixon appointees were dissenting from the majority opinion when they sided with Goss. The majority opinion stated that the due process clause did, in fact, guarantee Lopez the right to a hearing before his suspension.

It is true that the Court indicated that they were only recommending some brief opportunity for future students to have a chance to explain that some kind of mistake was being made, rather than a full, formal hearing on the issue. They also stressed the impact that a lengthy suspension from high school could have on a student's future educational plans. Nonetheless, this case may well have been the high water mark for the liberal interpretation of due process of law. Surely there are very few cases wherein any court has given a broader view of what constitutes "fundamental fairness" than the *Goss v. Lopez* decision. However, if there was a peak in liberal influence on the Supreme Court in 1975, the final quarter of the 20th century has certainly seen a swing in the other direction.

If liberals tend to be excessively broad in their interpretation of due process, there are some striking examples in which conservatives take an excessively narrow interpretation. An interesting example of this came in the 1986 case of *Bowers v. Hardwick*:

Due Process For Gays?

An Atlanta police officer legally entered the bedroom of a gay man named Michael Hardwick. He found Hardwick engaging in the act of sodomy with another man. A Georgia statute made the act of sodomy (both homosexual and heterosexual) a felony that was punishable by one to twenty years in prison. Hardwick was arrested and charged with violating that section of the penal code. Hardwick brought his case to the U.S. Supreme Court in 1986 alleging, inter alia (among other things), that this law was fundamentally unfair, that the state of Georgia had no right to criminalize private sexual activity between freely consenting adults and therefore his rights under the due process clause had been violated.

Once again, the four Nixon appointees to the Court argued that the due process clause did not give gay individuals a right to engage in sodomy if a state legislature decided to make it illegal. However, this time they found the all-important fifth vote and the state of Georgia won the case. The Court's decision in this case would have widespread impact because twenty-five states make sodomy a crime, while the other twenty-five do not prohibit it. It is arguable that *Bowers v. Hardwick* represents the most narrow interpretation of due process.

The pivotal issue in the Bowers case was that the "majority of the Georgia electorate believes homosexual sodomy is immoral and unacceptable" and that the law "is constantly based on notions of morality." Therefore, Justice White concluded for the Supreme Court majority, the state of Georgia has the right to criminalize sodomy.

Today's college students appear to have a different view of homosexuality than their parents' generation. A 1998 Gallup poll reflected part of this difference when Gallup asked if homosexuality was immoral. While more than 70 percent of respondents over 65 years of age answered *yes*, less than half of the respondents in their 20s agreed.[1] So it is not surprising that students read the decision in the Bowers case and are generally shocked. Even those students who had previously argued that gays should not be allowed in the military tend to side with the right of adult gay individuals to do whatever they want in their own bedrooms. They ask, Where does the state get the right to tell people what kind of sex they can have? How can it be considered "fundamentally fair" to put some gay man in prison for twenty years simply for having sex with another man?

Even those students who found the *Goss v. Lopez* case to be an excessively broad interpretation of due process tend to disagree with the Court's decision in *Bowers*. These are students whose view of homosexuality is a product of their times. Most of them were born more than a decade after the incident at the Stonewall Inn where a police raid of the bar met with violent resistance and touched off the modern gay rights movement. Many have friends or family members who are "out of the closet." Frequently, a student will inquire whether or not heterosexual couples—indeed married couples—could be imprisoned for practicing particular forms of consensual sexual behavior in private. The answer is something they find incomprehensible.

When the Bowers case was first granted certiorari, a heterosexual married couple joined the suit. They claimed that they were planning on engaging in sodomy with each other and that the law infringed upon their right to do so. The Georgia Supreme Court dismissed their claim, however, saying that since they had not been arrested they lacked standing to bring this suit. The U.S. Supreme Court, therefore, did not have the opportunity to consider the claim of heterosexuals engaging in sodomy while hearing the Bowers case. However, as we shall see in Chapter 7, they would later hear such a case and they would once again approve the right of the government to punish people who engage in the "wrong kind" of sex.

The Court came a long way from the interpretation of due process that said Lopez had a right to a hearing before being suspended from high school, to an interpretation that said an individual does not have a constitutional right to touch his or her lover in a manner some others consider immoral. The overwhelming majority of today's students find these decisions shocking but at the extreme ends of the opposite sides of the political spectrum.

LIMITS ON GOVERNMENT INTERVENTION

There may be no more important question that can be asked of students considering the role of government than what, in the students' opinion, is the proper limit of government's power to intervene in the life of the individual. At what point has the state overreached its proper bounds in regulating behavior that should be none of its business? The answer to that question has changed over the past few decades.

Some students will quote John Stuart Mill: "My rights stop where your rights begin." As a young law professor, former New York Governor Mario Cuomo frequently used that quote in his lectures. However, once elected governor of New York, Cuomo signed a law that made it a crime for us to risk our lives by not buckling up a seatbelt. Do we not have a right to take such chances when no one else is endangered? Libertarian students take the position that the government has no right to restrict any action that does not endanger someone other than the person performing the act.

They will generally approve of laws that make it a crime to drive a car with a child inside who has not been properly secured in a car seat or a seatbelt because this is a form of child neglect. However, they do not recognize the right of the state to impose a similar penalty for failing to secure your own seatbelt. The government, they argue, has no right to protect us against our own foolishness.

The traditional test for determining the validity of state regulation of behavior is called "the compelling state interest test." Does the statute in question bear a reasonable relationship to some evil that the state is authorized to prevent? The state cannot punish people for not loving their neighbors. The state *can* punish them for burning down their neighbor's house. Outlawing drunk driving has an obvious goal that no one would question. How about outlawing wearing blue shirts on Sundays? Would such a statute be considered constitutional?

William Blackstone made this distinction a decade before the American Revolution. In his renowned *Commentaries*, published between 1765 and 1769, and enormously influential on the thinking of the framers, Blackstone wrote, "Laws should not regulate and constrain our conduct in matters of mere indifference, without any good end in view." But what constitute matters of "mere indifference?"

Blackstone gives two examples—one legitimate and the other unjustified by any governmental interest. Both had been passed by the English Parliament at the request of an English king. The first law required that every deceased Englishman be buried in a wool suit. The second law prohibited the use of "pikes" on men's shoes (a pike was a kind of high heel). Blackstone argued that the first law was defensible and the second law was not. Most students argue that neither law makes any sense and that both of them should be nullified by the court if anyone should challenge them. Where is the "compelling state interest" in either of these situations?

The underlying reason for the ban on pikes was that the king personally found them effeminate and did not like to see men wearing them. The requirement of the wool suit, however, was designed to boost the British wool industry, which had fallen on hard times. A temporary slowdown in the demand for wool threatened sheep ranchers with bankruptcy. When the demand for wool increased, prices soared because the ranchers could not supply the market. In Blackstone's reasoning, the protection of an industry is the proper role of government; the implementation of the king's personal tastes in dress was not.

Thomas Jefferson said that it mattered not whether his neighbor believed in one god or twenty gods—it neither picked his pocket nor broke his leg. In other words, for Jefferson as well as Blackstone, a law that is not directed at some compelling state interest or that has no rational relationship to some legitimate state goal is a law that is arbitrary and therefore a deprivation of liberty. And such laws—even when based on the will of a democratically elected majority—should be struck down as a denial of due process.

In the Bowers case, the state of Georgia did not argue that there was any compelling state interest other than the public's interest in preventing "immoral behavior." This came as something of a surprise to Court watchers. Keep in mind that Michael Hardwick was arrested in 1982 and his case reached the Court in 1986. During those four years, the news carried an ever-increasing number of reports about a dreaded new disease that seemed to be both fatal and untreatable, as well as being centered among gay males.

Was there a "compelling state interest" in preventing the spread of AIDS? Of course. Is it possible that laws prohibiting homosexual sodomy could help restrict the spread of AIDS? The argument was never made. The Court's majority opinion ignored any public health argument and concentrated simply on the immorality of the act. Yet it's troubling to ague that "immorality" as the basis of a "compelling state interest" justifies criminalizing particular activities. If we added up the number of activities that were considered "immoral" in Blackstone's days and added in the number of things still considered "immoral" in certain fundamentalist nations, the list would be enormous. Intermarriage between different races was once considered "immoral." So were smoking, drinking and dancing among some religious sects. If politically incorrect jokes are deemed "immoral," could telling them in public be made a felony under a state penal code? Where does it end?

CONCLUSION

This chapter has looked at legal dilemmas that grow out of the "establishment clause" of the First Amendment, as well as the "equal protection" clause and the "due process" clause of the Fourteenth Amendment. It has examined students' opinions about such things as statutory rape, the constitutional rights of suspended high school students and the rights of gays to have sex. Clearly, the Bill of Rights covers a wide range of human activities and many of the dilemmas raised by these rights result in differences of opinion about the proper solution. Differences of opinion are a part of the fabric of life. As a nation, we struggle with the concept of what *equal* means in a diverse society and whose voices will be represented in the search for that definition. For students, a discussion of due process is an opportunity to examine not only the perspectives of some of these voices, but the reasoning processes that help us arrive at a just decision.

NOTE

1. G. Gallup, *The Gallup Poll Monthly* (Princeton, NJ: The Gallup Poll, July 28, 1998).

SUGGESTED READINGS

Alley, R. (Ed.). (1999). *The Constitution & religion: Leading Supreme Court cases on church and state.* Amherst, NY: Prometheus Books.

Berger, R. (1989). *The fourteenth amendment and the Bill of Rights.* Tulsa: University of Oklahoma Press.

Dewey, J. (1909). *Moral principles in education.* Boston: Houghton Mifflin.

Fallon, S.L. (1996). *The Bill of Rights: What it is, what it means and how it's been misused.* Irvine, CA: Dickens Press.

Kennedy, C. & Alderman, E. (1992). *In our defense: The Bill of Rights in action.* NY: Avon Books.

Rossum, R. A. & Tarr, G.A. (1995). *American Constitution: The Bill of Rights and subsequent amendments.* New York: Bedford Books.

Rudolph, S. (1993). *The philosophy of freedom: The ideological origin of the Bill of Rights.* New York: University Press of America.

Chapter 6

Crime

To debate the underlying morality of crime and punishment we need accurate information, not media distortions. Are we overly soft on violent criminals, overly punitive with nonviolent criminals, or possibly both?

A discussion of the underlying morality of penal codes should begin with two moral propositions. The first is that it would clearly be immoral for our system of justice to be excessively punitive; that is, to give a long prison sentence to an offender for littering the street with an empty coffee cup. The second is that it would be equally immoral to be excessively lenient with an offender and thereby fail to avenge the wrong that was done to his victim. Giving probation to a violent rapist, for instance, is a moral failure on our part to implement retributive justice. Presumably, everyone agrees with these two propositions. Unfortunately, that is usually where general agreement ends in any discussion of crime and punishment in America today.

There is probably no more divisive a question one can ask a class of college students today than the question of what should be done about the problem of serious crime. The solutions suggested range from the hard liners' demand for massive executions for violent offenders and imprisonment of every pot smoker, to the liberals' appeal for a war on poverty and job training programs for violent felons.

It is not surprising, of course, that college students should feel strongly about this subject. The nation as a whole sometimes seems obsessed with the subject. A poll taken in early 2000 showed that 71 percent of Americans believed that the subject of crime was either "very important" or "extremely important" in the forthcoming presidential election.[1] College students reflect this sentiment.

Yet students are under a number of serious misconceptions about the extent of the crime problem. So these misconceptions have to be cleared up or the discussion about solutions cannot progress very far. The crime rate in the United States is simply not as overwhelming as most students have been led to believe. With the exception of homicide, the rate of crime in the United States is not much different from that in the rest of the industrialized world. Moreover, the rate is substantially lower than it was at its peak in the late seventies. A little history is in order.

The FBI reported that the national rate of serious crime rose by a historically unprecedented 112 percent during the 1960s. It remained roughly the same throughout the 1970s and it started to drop in the 1980s. Between 1980 and 1997 the rate actually fell about 15 percent. (Actually, victimization studies suggest that the decline in the rate was more than double the fall reported by the FBI.)

The FBI relies on the willingness of people to report crime, rather than the cross-sectional surveys used in victimization studies. This can lead to major distortions, such as those caused by the 911 system. The implementation of the 911 emergency response system has dramatically changed the levels of reporting. In 1973, for instance, New York City introduced the 911 system along with a major public information campaign. The introduction of the system resulted in increases in reported robberies of 400 percent and in reported burglaries of 1,300 percent during the next two years. As the 911 system spread across the United States through the 1970s, similar increases could be anticipated. There is no way of knowing exactly how much additional crime was *reported* nationwide due to this new technology (as opposed to how much additional crime was *occurring*), but a look at the National Crime Victimization Survey suggests that the impact was substantial.

There is one criminal category in which the United States is ahead of all the other industrialized nations. American homicide rates are higher than in any other industrialized nation and always have been. But over-all crime rates in all other serious offenses tend to be about the same. (England actually has a burglary rate that is significantly higher than the U.S. rate, and the rate of car theft per capita in France is higher than just about anywhere.) The vast majority of students are generally not aware of this and find it difficult to believe. While the *rate of crime* in the sixties began to soar as the baby boomers reached the crime-prone age group, Gallup polls at that time suggested that the *fear of crime* felt by the students of the sixties was actually less than it is today. Media coverage of crime stories is far more extensive today than it was in the sixties, and these stories have raised the level of fear about crime. This may account for a general shift to the right in the student opinions concerning what should be done about crime.

DEMOGRAPHICS

There is a need to spend a good deal of time discussing the myths and realities about crime rates in the United States with college students today. The extent of student confusion about the crime problem is very quickly apparent. The demographic explanation for the variation in national crime rates seems to come as the biggest surprise to students. This is probably because this is one of the few explanations for crime that does not involve the usual right-wing or left-wing myths about the problem of crime, and it is an explanation that the media seems to studiously avoid.

Almost all the class discussions dealing with the causes of crime take on an overwhelmingly polemical tone. People on the political left have a collection of dogmas to which they cling religiously and which is usually a fair match for the collection of dogmas held by those on the political right. The conservatives, of course, explain crime in terms of widespread moral breakdown and excessive leniency; the left cites as the root causes of crime the lack of opportunity for the poor and the racial discrimination that targets black males. Rarely, does either side even mention the demographic impact on crime rates, even though many criminologists believe that as much as 80 percent of all the variation in the rate of crime can be attributed to demographics. So there is usually a need to sketch some basics about what we know about crime statistics.

The FBI's Uniform Crime Reports (UCR) were started in 1932 and have, ever since, recorded the number of certain felonies—known as the index crimes—that are reported to American police each year. As noted above, between 1960 and 1970 the UCR showed a historically unprecedented increase of 112 percent in the rate of crime. At the time—and to some extent even today—the political right blamed the explosion in crime on everything from Supreme Court decisions restricting the powers of police to the growing counterculture with its subversive rock music, marijuana, and communes. The political left blamed the urban poverty of migrating African-Americans forced out of the South, moral outrage against the war in Vietnam, and the frustrations of the Civil Rights movement.

But without knowing any of these things were going to happen in the sixties, there were some scholars who were very accurately predicting the rise in crime during those years. When students attempt to predict the level of the American crime rate five or ten years from now, about a third of the students predict a higher crime rate; another third predict a decrease. The others admit they have no idea. It is helpful for them to consider an article written in 1955 about the forthcoming American crime rate.

How Did Norman Ryder Know What He Knew?

Norman Ryder was a professor at Princeton. In 1955 he wrote an article predicting that from 1960 until 1970 the rate of serious crime in the United States was going to increase at a pace that was historically unprecedented. The Uniform Crime Reports indicate that the rate of increase in the "index crimes" during the decade of the sixties was a historically unprecedented 112 percent.

Twenty years after Ryder wrote his article, it was possible to use his formula to predict that the crime rate in the United States would start falling in the early eighties and continue plummeting for at least fifteen years. An examination of the results of the National Crime Victimization Survey reveals that Professor Ryder's formula was once again correct.[2] How did Ryder know what he knew?

Ryder was a demographer. He counted people. Like all demographers, he knew that there are certain states of human life in which people are more likely to engage in various activities. There is a time to be born and a time to die and a time to fall in love. And a time to get involved in criminal activities. The ten years during which people are most likely to commit crimes are from fourteen to twenty-four years of age. It is not that involvement in crime never begins after one's twenty-fifth birthday; it is simply that it is very rare. Human beings—mostly males—disproportionately engage in criminal activities during the decade that they are part of the crime-prone age group of fourteen to twenty-four.

There is no better demonstration of this "disproportionate criminality" than the year 1975. It was in that year when the baby boomers had swelled the ranks of the crime-prone age group and an unprecedented 21 percent of the American population was between fourteen and twenty-four years of age. In that year, the FBI reported that of the roughly 2 million felony arrests made by American police, the percentage of the arrestees who were fourteen to twenty-four years of age was not 21 percent of the total group—as we would expect it to be if crime were equally distributed throughout all age groups. The percentage of all those arrested for felonies that year who were in the crime-prone age group was 74 percent.

In other words, almost three out of four felonies nationwide were attributable to a group that made up about one out of five Americans. What would happen if this group—referred to by Norman Ryder as the "army of barbarians"—was to suddenly decrease rapidly and become a much smaller percentage of the total population? When the babies born during the "birth dearth" of 1965 to 1980 entered the fourteen- to twenty-four-year-old age group, would we not see a dramatic decrease in crime? Would we not anticipate an extraordinary drop in crime in the 1990s?

Examination of a birth chart showing the number of live births in the United States in this century is very revealing. With a calculator it can be seen that in 1960 there were 29 million people in this age group but by 1970 that figured had swelled to 41 million. By 1995 this number had fallen to 32 million and the crime rate was falling rapidly everywhere. It would have been a miracle if we had not experienced a boom in crime when the baby boomers hit the crime-prone age group in the sixties, and it would have been equally baffling if the "birth dearth" babies born between 1965 and 1980 were able to keep the crime rate as high as it had been. The most ironclad rule of criminology has to be this: If a baby isn't born in the first place, he is not going to steal your hubcaps fourteen years later.

Put another way, when the fourteen- to twenty-four-year-olds constituted 21 percent of the population in the late 1970s, crime rates hit their peak. When that age group fell to just 12 percent of the population in the mid-1990s, the rate fell. It had to. Regardless of increases in job opportunities or prison capacity, the crime rate will fall when the percentage of a nation's population between the ages of fourteen and twenty-four goes down.

The key question today is this: Where will the crime-prone age group be headed over the next decade or so? The answer is not encouraging. If we look at the birth rate over the past twenty-four years, we can see that in 2000 the number of people turning twenty-five are far fewer than the number of thirteen-year-olds who will turn fourteen. That is, those born in 1976 (3.1 million) and those born in 1986 (3.6 million) indicate that the army of barbarians will grow by half a million.

So what can be done about the possibility of future increases in the crime rate? Should we continue with the "get tough" approach in order to prevent the increase in crime that demographers imply is inevitable? And, if so, what specific steps can be taken to help fight crime?

In general, today's students have numerous suggestions for how to deal with crime. Unfortunately, many of these ideas mirror the superficial discussions of crime that are heard on talk shows, and very often the ideas are not very well thought out. Three or four suggestions appear again and again in class discussions about crime.

The first suggestion is almost always to build more prisons. The second most common suggestion is to do away with plea bargaining and parole. And, finally, students argue that there should be fewer constitutional rights for individuals who are charged with a crime. Since there is considerable confusion about these areas, it is important for students to distinguish between the myths and the realities that underlie public policy on crime.

MORE PRISONS?

In the last two decades there has been an unprecedented increase in the use of imprisonment in the United States. This expansion of the imprisonment rate did not happen in the other Western democracies and, it happened very unevenly among the fifty states. The increase in imprisonment rates per 100 thousand population among the fifty states between 1972 and 1992 ranged from a low of 55 percent in West Virginia to a high of 690 percent in Delaware. While crime rates have fallen in every state during the past two decades, the rate at which the fall has occurred has been the same in the states that invested in massive prison expansion as it has been in the states that did not expand their rate of imprisonment.[3] So, if building more prisons doesn't reduce crime, what good are prisons, and how much more should we invest in building and maintaining them?

It would appear that the U.S. public is largely unaware of how many "petty offenders" are being held in the nation's prisons. A recent study on the seriousness of the crimes for which prison inmates are serving time in the United States is informative. As part of the study, a poll was taken of adult Americans. It was called "National Estimate of the Severity of Crimes Committed by Persons Admitted to State and Federal Prisons."[4] The poll was done to determine what kinds of crimes the respondents considered to be "very serious crimes," "serious crimes," "moderate crimes," and "petty crimes." The researchers then compared the respondents' characterization of crimes to the offenses for which the nation's inmates were imprisoned.

They found that 52 percent of inmates were serving time for what the poll indicated were considered "petty crimes"; 29 percent were imprisoned for "moderate crimes"; only 14 percent for "serious crimes"; and 4 percent for "very serious crimes." Yet the public hears conflicting information from the advocates of more prisons. Consider, for instance, Princeton University criminologist John DiIulio's argument against extending alternative programs for convicted offenders. In his widely acclaimed work, *No Escape: The Future of American Corrections*, DiIulio states:

> Ninety-five percent of prisoners are violent offenders, repeat offenders (having two or more felony convictions), or violent repeat offenders; under 5 percent of prisoners can be meaningfully characterized as minor, petty or low-risk offenders.[5]

His statement leaves the impression that the vast majority of inmates are dangerous, violent criminals who should not be dealt with outside prison walls. This claim has been widely repeated in the media—including the editorial page of the *Wall Street Journal*—and in academia and it deserves better scrutiny.

The Bureau of Justice Statistics in the U.S. Department of Justice reports that for every one hundred individuals admitted to state prisons annually, only around 27 percent have been convicted of a violent offense. The others are property offenders (34 percent), drug offenders (29 percent), and public order offenses (7 percent).[6] How can we square these figures with what DiIulio claims?

The truth is that almost everyone who goes to prison is a "repeat offender" but not necessarily also "violent." Almost no one goes to *prison* for a first offense. At best, they may go to county jail for up to a year, but anyone who goes to prison has to be sentenced for more than a year. If you think about it, that 5 percent who are nonviolent *and* nonrepeat offenders must have stolen an enormous amount of money or sold an enormous amount of drugs in order to get a *prison* sentence for their first offense. When DiIulio says 95 percent are *"violent or repeat"* of-fenders, he fails to mention that almost all first-time felony convictions for property or drug offenses result in either probation or a *jail* sen-tence for a year or less. They do not ordinarily draw a *prison* sentence, which, by definition, must involve a term of more than a year.

Of course, murderers and rapists will usually draw first-offense *prison* terms but, taken together, they make up only about 1 percent of all of-fenders. In other words, the vast majority of people sent to prison have more than one felony conviction; that is, they are "repeat" offenders, but that in no way implies that they are "violent." Individuals previ-ously convicted of writing a bad check or of having stolen a car years ago could get a prison term for selling marijuana. But that makes them "re-peat" offenders, as DiIulio points out. However, the impression he leaves with his readers is that such individuals are also violent and are too dangerous to be dealt with outside prison walls. Arguing that 95 percent are "violent or repeat" offenders is like arguing that they are "violent or right-handed" offenders. It is very misleading.

DiIulio notwithstanding, the United States imprisons an extraordi-nary number of nonviolent offenders and the public is, by and large, unaware of the extent to which their tax dollars are being used to incar-cerate nonviolent prisoners. Most students simply refuse to believe that federal courts are actually giving more time to the average drug dealer than they give to the average murderer. But it is true. In 1992, federal prisons held 1,800 people convicted of murder for an average time served of 4.5 years.[7] This compared with 12,727 nonviolent first-time drug offenders held in federal prison for an average time served of 6.5 years.[8]

Very often, drug offenders with no history of violence are sent to an already crowded prison that can only make room for them by paroling some other inmates—perhaps child molesters or rapists. With an esti-mated 12 million users of hard drugs in the United States, and perhaps three times as many pot smokers, imprisonment is clearly not the an-swer to the drug problem. In point of fact, the United States is the only nation today that is still trying to lock up its drug problem. Prisons in other countries are more likely to be reserved for serious predators.

Most college students today are very skeptical about the so-called war on drugs even before they look at the statistics on imprisonment. Once they have the opportunity to examine the actual patterns of pun-ishment, they most often conclude that prison space would be better used to extend the sentences of violent offenders and alternatives should be found for nonviolent property and drug offenders. They believe that murderers should never be paroled and sex offenders should be held for longer periods than they currently serve. For the most part, after examining the appropriate data, they conclude that we are generally too lenient on violent offenders while treating nonviolent offenders with disproportionate severity.

PLEA BARGAINING AND PAROLE

A second argument frequently made by students today is that the criminal justice system is overly lenient on criminals through a combination of plea bargaining and parole. While these students appear to be aware of how extensive plea bargaining and parole are in today's criminal justice system, they are still very uninformed about how the system actually works.

The political popularity of "getting tough on crime" is readily evidenced by the fact that one state after another has modified or eliminated parole, and restricted the practice of plea bargaining. To drive the point home, recent federal legislation mandates that unless a state requires that convicted offenders serve at least 85 percent of their sentences, that state will be denied federal criminal justice assistance. (Of course, a state could simply change its penal code to provide a sentence that is half of the current time, then require that the inmate serve 85 percent of that time. Such a move would completely circumvent the purpose of the Truth in Sentencing Act.) Plea bargaining and parole should be understood for what they really are.

Every day prosecutors all over the country negotiate with armed robbers for a guilty plea and they are forced to "swallow the gun"; that is, lessen the charge to unarmed robbery and concomitantly reduce the punishment to perhaps half of what the penal code demands for those guilty of armed robbery. Many conservative legislators as well as many college students have argued that this process should be stopped. Others hold that this process is far less harmful than it seems.

Assume that the people of a state are polled about the appropriate punishment for a given offense. Since there is a finite amount of incarceration time that the taxpayers are willing to pay for, any increase in "inmate years" for, say, burglary, must sooner or later be balanced by a reduction in "inmate years" elsewhere, for example, among child molesters or rapists. We simply cannot afford to keep every offender behind bars for all time. Tough choices are necessary.

Therefore, let us suppose that the voters are polled and are asked how much time behind bars they feel is "fair" for specific crimes. For example, how many years or months or weeks should an individual convicted of "unarmed robbery" serve? (Robbery is the taking of personal property through force or fear; armed robbery—especially with a gun—is ordinarily punished much more severely than robberies committed without a weapon.)

Let us assume that the voters indicate to their political leaders that they feel it is "fair" for an unarmed robber to serve two years behind bars. That is actually *serve* that time—not get early release through parole, not plea bargain the sentence down from two-years and not receive a two year suspended sentence, but rather to live behind bars for twenty-four months. How do we best implement the will of the voters in this case?

The hard-line reformers say that we have to "get tough" with criminals by seeing to it that they serve longer terms. Assume that they are correct. Assume that on average American prison sentences are presently too short and that we should increase the time served. How does a state legislature most effectively increase the time served by convicted criminals? Those who say "abolish plea bargaining and parole" should do a cost-benefit analysis of the system as it actually functions.

Let's say that at present the penal code of a state calls for two years as punishment for unarmed robbery. When Danny, the defendant, is charged with unarmed robbery and is brought to justice, he is likely to be told that if a jury convicts him he will get the maximum the law allows; that is, two years. However, if he is willing to save us the money and trouble of a trial, we will find it in our hearts to reduce his sentence to one year. In point of fact, something close to 90 percent of all felony convictions nationwide come from such plea bargains. If we are required to convict these people through criminal trials instead of guilty pleas, we will need something like nine times as many criminal courts—at a staggering cost.

When Danny arrives at the state prison door, the warden is likely to ask that he behave himself during his stay in prison; cooperate with the staff, avoid conflict with other inmates, and do his time peacefully. American wardens have around 700,000 correctional officers to tend to the roughly 2 million people held in prisons and jails. If they are unable to persuade the average inmate to cooperate with their staff, it is likely they will need a substantial increase in the ratio of staff to inmates. The cost of prisons is already staggering; personnel costs are by far the biggest part of a prison budget. Increases in prison staff in order to control inmates would add greatly to the cost of incarceration.

So, as a way of inducing cooperative behavior from Danny, the warden is likely to point out that the state offers early parole, for example, a day off for every day he stays out of trouble. The bottom line is that Danny will be home in six months and he will become an example of the "lenience" which, we are told, can only be avoided through the abolition of plea bargaining and parole.

In fact, most state legislators are well aware of this situation. Every year they have the opportunity to revise the state penal code and change the amount of time given for robbery; in fact, it is very likely that they already have. The likelihood is that a good percentage of the legislators in any given state were once district attorneys who prosecuted armed robbers and know exactly what goes on. And that is why they long ago inflated the sentence for armed robbery (and every other offense) so as to make allowances for our current cost-effective system.

It is likely that if a state really wants an offender to actually serve two years in prison, legislators will specify in their penal code a punishment of, say, eight years. That way, the prosecutor can "bargain" with the obviously guilty to get them to waive their right to a jury trial and plead guilty in exchange for half the sentence, that is, four years.

Of course, when the warden explains the state's parole policy, it will become obvious to the inmate that it is in his interest to behave himself in prison, thereby saving the taxpayer the cost of hiring many additional correctional officers. So, in essence, he will only serve two years—the time thought appropriate by the voters in the first place. And if the voters feel that two years is insufficient, then the answer is for the penal code to be revised again. It is this "arbitrary inflation" of the penal code sentences that allows the system to be both sufficiently punitive and at the same time cost-effective.

It simply requires the doubling of the time threatened for a particular crime to result in a doubling of the actual time served. The alternative of stripping away the ability of the prosecutor and the warden to deal in a cost-effective way with defendants and inmates comes from those who just do not understand how the criminal justice system works. And the suggestion that plea bargaining and parole lead to lenient treatment of offenders is one more myth about the American justice system.

CONSTITUTIONAL PROTECTIONS FOR CRIMINALS?

For the most part, today's college students are far more in favor of "getting tough" on crime than their counterparts of the sixties. Oddly enough, this attitude comes after three decades of getting more and more "tough" on crime. In 1968, Richard Nixon was elected president with a promise to "get tough" on crime. He argued in his campaign that he would appoint "tough, law-and-order" justices to the U.S. Supreme Court and they would "strictly construe" the Constitution so as to curtail the rights of criminals. The idea was that by reducing the constitutional protections given to criminals, we could reduce overall levels of crime.

Virtually every political campaign since then has emphasized the importance of "getting tough" on crime. There may be no better evidence of this get-tough policy than the fact that on the day Nixon left office there were just over 300,000 inmates in America's jails and prisons. Today, even though the National Crime Victimization Survey of the Department of Justice indicates that the crime rate is lower than when Nixon left office, there are about 2 million inmates, more than six times as many as 1974.

Laws have been toughened; sentences have been increased; hard-line, conservative justices have been appointed to the High Court and the definition of "due process of law" has been narrowed in numerous Supreme Court decisions. Some now argue that it has been narrowed too much. Some suggest that the process has gone too far and that the anticrime net being cast by law enforcement has become wider than a free society should allow. Students consider the moral aspects of the extremes to which this "get tough" approach has gone and, for the most part, they are shocked at cases like the recent Supreme Court decision in the Bennis case:

An Errant Husband Borrows Her Car

State "forfeiture laws" require an individual convicted of certain crimes to "forfeit" any personal property used in the crime, this in addition to the penalty prescribed by law. These laws have been very popular with Congress and state legislators over the last two decades. In an attempt to curtail prostitution, the state of Michigan passed a forfeiture law mandating that any car driven by a suspect who solicits an act of prostitution be forfeited to the state. John Bennis took his wife's car and, without her knowledge, solicited a prostitute. He was arrested. The car was seized and the court ruled that it would be forfeited to the state. Mrs. Bennis challenged the constitutionality of this law, arguing that seizing her property because of her husband's transgressions was a denial of due process of law.

The U.S. Supreme Court heard the case in 1996 (116 S. Ct. 994, 1996). The issue was this: Was the state of Michigan denying due process of law to Mrs. Bennis by seizing her property even though she had committed no crime?

When students consider this case, the majority are outraged by the unfairness of punishing the wife for the sins of the husband. They argue that the state of Michigan has gone too far in its "get tough" campaign and that the Supreme Court should strike down that forfeiture law. Everyone in the class seems surprised when informed that the U.S. Supreme Court, in a decision written by Chief Justice William Rehnquist, ruled in favor of Michigan, concluding that this was not unfair to Mrs. Bennis and, therefore, not a denial of due process. The owner of the car, they concluded, should be more careful about whom she lends it to. Clearly, criminal penalties in the United States have indeed seen the effect of the "get tough" policies introduced by Richard Nixon and, for the most part, college students are starting to have reservations about how far they should go.

If the government's seizure of Mrs. Bennis's car disturbs students, the government's attempt to regulate sexual behavior infuriates them. It may well be that the biggest attitudinal change between the students of thirty years ago and those of today has to do with sexual behavior. The majority of students today are invariably surprised that sexual behavior between freely consenting adults is a criminal act in some states. In fact, there remain eleven states and the military where the penal code makes oral sex a criminal offense, even when carried out by married, freely consenting adults in the privacy of their bedroom. Naturally, there are very few prosecutions for this offense, but it does happen, and to contemporary college students it is mind boggling that any government anywhere in this day and age could possibly have the power to imprison someone for such an act. Consider the case of Nicholas Johnson:

Must Foreplay Be Government Approved?

Nicholas Johnson, a member of the U.S. Air Force, was dating a woman with whom he was having sex. Their relationship included oral sex. All of their sexual activities were conducted off the base and on Johnson's free time. (Johnson was not married to the woman, but the law would have been no different even if he had been.)

After Johnson broke up with the woman, she reported these activities to his commanding officer and he was arrested and prosecuted for the crime of having a type of sex that is made criminal by the Air Force. He was convicted and sentenced to a year in jail. He appealed his conviction to the U.S. Supreme Court, arguing that a year in prison for this behavior was clearly unfair. The Court allowed the defendant's felony conviction to stand, finding no violation of his right to due process of law.

There are very few moral debates in college classrooms that provoke the kind of consensus that this case does. Students are virtually unanimous in their belief that no government in a free society should have the power to prosecute and punish Nicholas Johnson. Many are shocked that his girlfriend was not also prosecuted, but most take the position that any type of sexual contact that two freely consenting adults engage in should be none of the government's business.

Liberal students argue for the right of individuals to maximize their freedom; conservative students argue for the proper limits of governmental control. Virtually all of them believe these sexual regulation laws should be changed.

NOTES

1. G. Gallup, *The Gallup Poll Monthly* (Princeton, NJ: The Gallup Poll, January 19, 2000).

2. U.S. Department of Justice, *Sourcebook of criminal justice statistics, 1991* (Washington, DC: Bureau of Justice Statistics, 1992), ch. 6.

3. J.D. Davey, *The politics of prison expansion: Winning elections by waging war on crime* (Westport, CT: Praeger, 1998).

4. J. Austin, & J. Irwin, *Who goes to prison?* (San Francisco: National Council on Crime and Delinquency, 1991).

5. I. DiIulio, *No escape: The future of American corrections* (New York: Basic Books, 1991), 4.

6. U.S. Department of Justice, *Bureau of justice statistics national update,* vol. 2, no. 2 (Washington, DC: Bureau of Justice Statistics, 1992), ch. 6.

7. U.S. Department of Justice, Bureau of Justice Statistics, *Federal criminal case processing, 1982–1991: With preliminary data for 1992* (Washington, DC: U.S. Government Printing Office: 18, Table 18, November 1993).

8. U.S. Department of Justice, *An analysis of non-violent drug offenders with minimal criminal histories* (Washington, DC: U.S. Government Printing Office, February 4, 1994).

SUGGESTED READINGS

Clear, T.R. (1994). *Harm in American penology: Offenders, victims and their communities*. Albany: SUNY Press.

Currie, E. (1985). *Confronting crime: An American challenge*. New York: Pantheon Books.

———. (1993). *Reckoning: Drugs, the cities and the American future*. New York: Hill and Wang.

Gibbons, D.C. (1992). *Society, crime and criminal behavior*. (6th ed.). Englewood Cliffs, NJ: Prentice-Hall.

Gordon, D. (1991). *The justice juggernaut*. New Brunswick, NJ: Rutgers University Press.

Inciardi, J.A. (1996). *Criminal justice*. (5th ed.). New York: Harcourt Brace College Publishers.

Kappeler, V.E., Blumberg, M., & Potter, G.W. (2000). *The mythology of crime and criminal justice* (3rd ed.). Prospect Heights, IL: Waveband Press.

Pepinsky, H.E., & Jesilow, P. (1984). *Myths that cause crime*. Washington, DC: Seven Locks Press.

Tonry, M. (1995). *Malign neglect*. New York: Oxford University Press .

———. (1996). *Sentencing matters*. New York: Oxford University Press.

Wilson, J.Q. (1975). *Thinking about crime*. New York: Basic Books.

Chapter 7

Poverty

Welfare reform or welfare repeal? Hunger next door to billion-aires.

SOCIAL JUSTICE

The United States has more billionaires than any other nation on earth. The current economy is the strongest of all the industrialized nations and stronger than it has been in many years. Unemployment and infla-tion have reached record low numbers and the federal budget actually shows a surplus. However, income inequality is probably greater today than at any other time in the past century. The top 20 percent in family income make about half the national income. In other words, the top one-fifth earns as much as the remaining 80 percent of families com-bined.

By official estimates, there are almost 40 million people in the United States living in poverty—about three-quarters of a million of them are homeless. A little more than one in five children in the United States live below the poverty level, which means that they are likely to go hungry on a regular basis. The president of Walt Disney, Inc., on the other hand, earns about a million dollars a day—seven days a week, fifty-two weeks a year.

In 1998 Congress and the president cut about $10 billion from future food stamp budgets while other political officials were authorizing new prison construction budgets totaling another $10 billion. When Richard Nixon left office in 1974, the number of black inmates in the United States was a little over 100,000. Today it is closing in on a million and in California over 42 percent of all black males in their twenties are currently under the control of the criminal justice system.

About three out of four children who qualify for Head Start programs are turned away because there are not enough tax dollars to accept them. The cost of incarcerating a single nonviolent offender is enough to pay for about fifteen four-year-olds for a year in a Head Start program.

Drug treatment programs are so scarce that more addicts are turned away from treatment than are accepted. Elected officials argue that drug treatment is too expensive, but we incarcerate around 400,000 drug offenders at a phenomenal cost.

In a world where the economy is rapidly transforming in extraordinary and unpredictable ways, the moral obligation to deal with poverty becomes more complex than ever before. What moral obligation is there for the "privileged" in American society today to help the underprivileged climb out of poverty?

Both the causes of and the cure for poverty are subjects that prompt heated discussions in college classrooms. For the most part, students who call for a more equal distribution of the nation's wealth are charged with trying to revive class struggle. Students who argue that inequalities of wealth are the natural outgrowth of inequalities in talent or effort are accused of insensitivity. Naturally, no one is in favor of poverty. There is a unanimous view that poverty is a problem that we would be better off without, although there is confusion about the extent to which it exists in our land of abundance. The question that separates students is this: Is there a moral obligation to eliminate poverty and, if so, how much should the government do in order to achieve that goal?

Generally, students tend to explain poverty in one of two ways: A minority see it as an outgrowth of the changing economic and social conditions that provide very narrow opportunities for those with limited education. The other side—generally, the majority, sees it in terms of self-destructive behavior on the part of the individual; that is, laziness, substance abuse, and irresponsible sexual behavior. Much of the debate bounces back and forth between those who see social programs as useful help for the needy and those who view them as wasteful excuses for careless behavior.

The former group echoes the views of the leftists of the sixties, whose sentiments dominated the debate over poverty at that time, and whose support undergirded Lyndon Johnson's war on poverty. The latter group often expresses fears about their own economic prospects. These students came of age after the Golden Age of the American economy had come to an end in the early seventies. Many of them grew up watching their parents get downsized or relocated by employers who seemed to owe them less loyalty than earlier generations had shown to their workers. They worry about their own futures and are skeptical about government's ability to help the poor.

It should be remembered that many of them spent their childhood in an America where the president regularly railed against the "waste, fraud, and abuse" of government poverty programs and about the "welfare queen" shopping with food stamps in her fur coat. The idea that poverty and homelessness were freely "chosen" was an idea that enjoyed the moral support of the White House throughout much of the eighties. Many of these middle class students have had very little, if any, personal contact with welfare families. A colleague of ours tells of a personal experience with a welfare family, which gets a strong reaction from students.

The Davises of Grand Street

Sharon Davis was an alcoholic welfare mother who had six children in a twelve-year period. There were at least three, and probably four, different fathers involved and each time Sharon gave birth her AFDC check was increased (about $75 in today's dollars). Her two oldest children, Victor and Anthony, grew up in a roach- and rodent-infested slum just off Grand Street on the lower east side of Manhattan. Growing up, they had very little supervision, very few meals, clothes, or protection from the numerous dangers of the neighborhood. In their adolescent years they held up a seventy-year-old man with a knife and stabbed him to death.

Our colleague knew Victor and Anthony Davis for five years before the murder. From the day he first met them, he suspected that one day they would wind up seriously harming someone. He still doesn't know how he could have prevented it.

In the neighborhood where he grew up, the only black people he was likely to see were house cleaners or gardeners. The idea that just a dozen miles away a ghetto like Harlem or the South Bronx could exist was never suggested to him or his friends. That made it all the more shocking to him when he got out of college and found a job working as a youth counselor on the streets of Harlem and, later, the lower east side of Manhattan.

The teenagers he was working with were not only from poor families, they were cut off from the rest of society. Working for a program funded by the Office of Economic Opportunity, he and his colleagues were called "detached street club workers." The idea was for them to contact teens who were out of school, out of work, and generally out of contact with their families, churches, and community. They were charged with the responsibility of introducing themselves and persuading them to drop into a "street club" that they had formed by renting a storefront or a community center and setting up a ping-pong table or a pool table, if they could find one. As these unconnected teenagers came in to see the youth counselor—even if it was just to get out of the cold—they received counseling about jobs or a graduate equivalency diploma (GED) program or getting into the service. A typical client would tell him that he wanted to go into the army but that he was on probation and the recruiting officer would not accept him until the probation officer released him from probation. And, naturally, the probation officer would not release him until the Army had accepted him. "How long has this been going on, Antoine?" he would ask. "Maybe six months?" It was the counselor's job to get them all together and clear up the red tape.

Two young kids attached themselves to him when he first started working there. They were too young to be part of his program but he would see a lot of them, and the depth of their poverty touched him deeply. Anthony and Victor Davis were eight and nine years old when he first met them. Anthony was an affable kid, always enthusiastic about running into the counselor and always trying to hit him up for a quarter or a dime or a nickel. "Hey, man, lemme hold a dollar. Lemme hold a dime. Come on, man."

Victor was more quiet. He was a sullen, angry kid. He would never ask for anything; in fact, he would never even take something the counselor offered him. If he bought Anthony a Coke, Victor would turn it down. Victor would steal anything he could find in the counselor's jacket if he laid it down and wasn't watching. But he would never accept a gift. He would spend a lot of time working with a shoeshine box trying to make some money. In all the times the counselor visited their apartment, he never saw food in their refrigerator. Every time he asked New York City social service workers to take these kids away from their neglectful mother, he would be told that they were not as bad off as other kids who were already clogging the system.

The building that they lived in had several abandoned apartments. Two of them were used regularly as "shooting galleries," where junkies could go and pay a guy with a gun a few dollars to protect their stash while they got high and nodded out. The smell of urine was always strong in the hallways. The Davises lived on the fourth floor. They had been thrown out of the public schools and they were supposed to be getting an instructor at home, but in all the years he knew them, the youth counselor never saw a teacher actually show up.

Hunger was a regular part of their lives. When they would walk past food stands that sold hot dogs, hamburgers, or pastilles, they would run their hand along the aluminum countertop and scoop up the spilled ketchup or mustard or relish and lick it off their hand. Once, he met them late at night with a box of popcorn. He had just come back from Washington, D.C., with three school buses filled with community activists who had gone to D.C. to protest cuts in the low-income housing budget. It was about two in the morning and he was headed toward his car when they spotted him. "Hey, man," they called out. They ran across the street and showed him a large carton filled with bags of popcorn. They offered him all he wanted—to take home to his kids, they suggested and named each one of his children They liked the idea of sharing their bounty with his children.

"Where did you get this stuff?" he demanded. "In the store, man. Down there." They were disappointed that he was not more grateful. "There are no stores open at two in the morning!" he argued. Victor responded defensively, "Them other guys broke in. Them big guys." The counselor stood there filled with middle-class righteousness telling them to just march themselves back up to that store and return that popcorn, but knowing in his heart that it may have been ten or twelve hours since they had eaten anything and that their next meal was less than certain. He went home.

During the summers there was an opportunity for these children to get out of Manhattan and spend a week on a lake upstate. It was called something like "the Fresh Air Fund," and the program required that the kids have two new T-shirts and a pair of sneakers. Anthony did not have sneakers so the counselor called the Welfare Department. The bureaucracy was overwhelming. Rather than just buying him a pair of sneakers

out of his own pocket he decided to see how nightmarish it could become to deal with the New York City Welfare Department. It took him
six weeks and about a dozen phone calls for Anthony to get his sneakers.

About a month after the boys came home from camp the same counselor was in a storefront shooting pool with a couple of kids. Anthony
was lining up a shot when the counselor looked down and saw the can-
vas on his left sneaker was all ripped and shredded. He chastised the
boy. "What is the matter with you, Anthony? Look at those sneakers!
You finally get a nice pair of sneakers and that's how you take care of
them?" He was determined to instill a little middle-class guilt. Anthony
looked down at his foot and nodded his head. "Yeah," he said mat-
ter-of-factly, "the rats got them." The image of an eight-year-old boy
sleeping in bed with rats gnawing at his sneakers under his bed is an image this man has never been able to shake. For him, it is the quintessen-
tial image of poverty in America.

They killed a seventy-year-old man. The New York *Daily News*
couldn't use their names because they were still minors. The paper
called them a "wolf pack." There were five of them. They had sur-
rounded the man in a building that the counselor was familiar with and
when he saw the story in the paper he knew he would know at least
some of them. Two of the boys he did not know, but it was Victor who
held the knife to the man. He had given them forty cents and Victor
had run the knife into his heart. The counselor never saw the Davis boys
again. They were sent to Wiltwick, a state training school. When he
spoke of the incident that night with his wife, she pointed out that the
Davis boys would have breakfast the next day. And a shower. And a bedroom without rats. And teachers.

The reaction of students to this story has changed over the years.
Twenty years ago there was a good deal of sympathy for the plight of
the Davis boys and support for the idea that government programs
should be devised that would improve the conditions under which they
were raised. Today's students are more inclined to grow angry at the
welfare system. Why, they ask, were these children not taken away from
Sharon Davis? Why was she subsidized every time she had another
out-of-wedlock birth? What were they thinking when they devised this
public policy?

The idea of jobs programs, housing, health care, or the adoption of a
livable wage survives only on the fringe of college classes today. There is
little sympathy for the Sharon Davises of the world. Her behavior is
seen as self-destructive and she is viewed as a lost soul who is beyond the

ability of the government to assist. How do they feel about the "working poor?" Are they more deserving of government help?

For the most part, today's college students are not very familiar with the number of the working poor in the United States and they have little understanding of the problems these people face. These are, after all, college students whose parents are for the most part relatively well educated. The rapidly changing realities of the "new economy" and the growing income gap between the educated and uneducated are things that most students are only vaguely aware of. A good example of the extent of changes in the economy is a dilemma that has faced all generations: an untimely pregnancy facing a young, low-wage couple.

The Blessed Event

Benny and Rhonda are twenty-year-old high school dropouts. They earn a minimum wage and they realize that without the ability to get further education, they will probably never earn more than low wages. They have dated for six months and Rhonda is now expecting a baby. Benny considers his three options to be abortion, abandonment, and marriage. He would like to marry Rhonda but wonders what life will be like raising a family on minimum wages, or wages just somewhat above that. His uncle Jack tells him that twenty-five years ago he was in exactly the same position, that he married Benny's aunt Maggie and that he has been happy ever since. Does Benny face the same future as Uncle Jack?

In Uncle Jack's day, a couple who were employed full time at the minimum wage could not only rent an apartment in most areas of the country, but they could rent a house. With overtime and a down payment, they may have even been able to buy a house. In order to bring a family of three to the "poverty level" while working at the minimum wage, a worker in 1973 would have had to work just thirty-four hours a week. Faced with that prospect, Jack and Maggie may well have been inclined to marry and set up a household.

But "setting up a household" today is a very different challenge than it was a generation ago. During the last twenty-five years, the minimum wage has been eroded by inflation to an extraordinary degree. The $1.60 minimum wage paid in Richard Nixon's America would equate to almost $8.00 at the start of the new century. When we add to that the increased FICA deductions for Social Security taxes over that time period, it turns out that for Benny to lift himself and Rhonda and the baby above the poverty level today, he would have to work fifty-two hours a week at the minimum wage. Whereas Uncle Jack needed to put in just thirty-four hours; Benny will need fifty-two hours in order to reach the poverty level and many more to inch ahead. In too many cases, that option is so discouraging that the household is not being set up and the out-of-wedlock birth rate continues to soar.

It is clear that the working poor today face a far more daunting challenge than their counterparts of a generation ago. Moreover, there are a lot more people who have fallen into the ranks of the "working poor." The number of Americans living under the poverty level increased over 50 percent in the last quarter of the 20th century (from about 25 million to about 40 million).

While the number of welfare recipients has declined rapidly in recent years, the number of working poor has grown. This has to do with two phenomena: (1) the increase in part-time jobs accepted by workers who would prefer full-time jobs but cannot find them and (2) the falling purchasing power of hourly wages.

The economic prospects for a large proportion of young, poorly educated people have dimmed to the point where starting a family is simply out of the question. A growing number of low-wage workers will never be able to support a family in the way that the last generation did. High school graduation was once some kind of guarantee of a decent-paying job and today we have a graduation rate of almost 85 percent. Unfortunately, an increasing number of entry-level jobs require more than merely a high school diploma.

Consider the numbers: Almost 30 percent of all workers in 1997 were employed in nonstandard (part-time or temporary) work arrangements. Hourly wages (in inflation-adjusted dollars) for private-sector employees from 1977 to 1994 actually fell 13.1 percent. For those without college degrees, it was even worse. The U.S. Census Bureau reports that between 1973 and 1989 the real income of male high school graduates dropped by a third.

A college degree has never been more important in the labor market than it is today. Wage gains for the top 20 percent have never been larger and most of that 20 percent is made up of college graduates (about 24 percent of American adults hold college degrees). But even a B.A. is no guarantee of financial success. More than 20 percent of college graduates will end up making less than the average high school graduate.

The problem is that the "new economy" brings such rapid change that it is difficult to keep up. Jobs have never been more plentiful but wages have been falling for half the work force. For many workers, skills once highly valued suddenly have become valueless. The promotional ladder of earlier generations has also disappeared. When companies hire a worker, they simply start him in another entry-level job, so that the gains in income from twenty-year-old high school grads to forty-year-old high school grads are much smaller than they used to be. More and more middle-aged workers are surviving on less than they made decades ago.

When today's college students look at these changes, they accept the idea that many of the old rules no longer apply in the quest for financial security. And they are eager to debate the causes of and cures for today's poverty. Conservative students are quick to ask, "Why are these people having babies?" They point out that the number of out-of-wedlock births has skyrocketed in recent decades and that single-parent families are naturally going to be more vulnerable to poverty. They blame a diminution in individual "character" in the last twenty years and suggest that today's young people do not have the same moral fiber as past generations.

Others respond that perhaps "moral fiber" is something that comes more easily when people have jobs with livable wages. Is it still true, they will ask, that anyone who is willing to work hard can make a decent living and support a family? MIT economist Lester Thurow estimates that a third of males in their twenties will never be able to earn enough to support a family. Liberal students will concede that some low-wage workers should act in a more morally responsible fashion but argue that it would be unrealistic to hope that all of them will ever develop the knowledge or talent necessary to hold anything but low-wage jobs. What will happen to people for whom the American dream of raising a family has become an illusion? Will inequality simply continue to grow as the globalization of trade continues to force American workers to compete with third-world workers? Should people be expected to deny themselves children because the economy has left them in its wake?

Students understand that the factory jobs once held by their uncles and fathers are now in the third world. The system of trade has become global and the jobs that their ancestors supported themselves with are never coming back. As globalization of the economy continues, national governments are shrinking in importance and global corporations constantly expand. The growth in inequality is occurring throughout the industrialized world, although the United States seems to be leading the way.

While there is little on the political or economic horizon that seems likely to bring about greater equality in the distribution of national wealth, there does seem to be a growing number of college students who are aware and concerned about the future of the working poor. Poverty, they frequently conclude, is not simply the result of moral failure. There are powerful currents in the global economy that are reducing the opportunities for millions of workers to enjoy the American dream.

These students also realize that things have never been better for the top 20 percent of American families who now make as much as the other 80 percent combined. It is clear to these students that educational level has never been as important in determining income as it is in the "new economy" and that only 24 percent of American adults are likely to ever earn a bachelor's degree. This augurs well for those college students who will complete their degree requirements but offers little hope for anything but growing inequality for those unable to achieve educational success.

SUGGESTED READINGS

Danziger, S., & Weinberg, D.H. (1986). *Fighting poverty: What works and what doesn't.* Cambridge, MA: Harvard University Press.

Dewey, J. (1899). *The school and society.* Chicago: University of Chicago Press.

Gilder, G. (1981). *Wealth and poverty.* New York: Basic Books.

Katz, M.B. (1986). *In the shadow of the poorhouse: A social history of welfare in America.* New York: Basic Books.

———. (1989). *The undeserving poor: From the war on poverty to the war on welfare.* New York: Pantheon Books.

Kaus, M. (1992). *The end of equality.* New York: Basic Books.

Krugman, P. (1992). *The age of diminished expectations: U.S. economic policy in the 1990's.* Cambridge, MA: MIT Press.

Meade, L. (1986). *Beyond entitlement.* New York: Free Press.

———. (1992). *The new politics of poverty.* New York: Basic Books.

Murray, C. (1984). *Losing ground: American social policy 1950–1980.* New York: Basic Books.

———. (1985). Helping the poor: A few modest proposals. *Commentary.*

Phillips, K. (1990). *The politics of rich and poor.* New York: Random House.

Chapter 8

Race

Colin Powell, Oprah Winfrey, Michael Jordan, Bill Cosby, Muhammad Ali and 51 percent of the prison population: *An American Dilemma*[1] continues.

A few years back, an editorial commented on a young African-American child who had discovered the Internet at a local library. After he had spent an enormous number of hours online, the librarian asked him why he was so excited about the Internet. The boy responded that he liked it so much "because it doesn't know I'm black."

When today's white college students hear about that child they frequently have a surprised reaction. How can a young African-American still be so fearful of racial discrimination? What can he be thinking of in a nation that has so successfully negotiated "the civil rights era" that it reveres Muhammad Ali, is practically begging General Colin Powell to run for president and is happy to pay a zillion dollars for Oprah Winfrey to share with us her values and her opinions about life in America? How could a black child come to fear racism in such a nation?

It is not easy to put oneself in the place of another. White students, who have grown up learning that the fight for civil rights was in the past, overwhelmingly express confidence that the battle was won. African-Americans they have shared classrooms with certainly seem to have benefited, they reason, and the rest just didn't take the opportunities handed to them. African-American students, however, usually take a very different position. How do we account for such a disconnect in perspective? More important, what do we do about it?

Many of those in the "helping" professions, particularly teachers, are not greatly representative of the cultures they serve. Their perspectives are shaded by their own experiences and it is possible that what the majority holds as true may be more a result of who the majority is than an accurate representation of reality. As we have seen, where we stand frequently depends on where we sit.

Often times, misunderstandings occur when one race, culture, religion, or gender interprets the experiences of the other. Inaccurate assumptions, based on subjective judgments, may thwart communication and exacerbate tensions in situations where the very purpose of the interaction is meant to be helpful. Such misinformation and one-sided thinking may have a devastating impact on those at the receiving end. For many students, viewing situations through the lens of another's experience provides a window to worlds that had previously been invisible. For those who exercise the power of the law (criminal justice officials at all levels) and for those who hold power over children (like teachers and social workers), a diverse outlook is essential.

Most white students do understand the importance of race, sharing the same concerns that the whole nation feels. A poll taken in January 2000 on the issues that were important for the 2000 presidential campaign showed that 56 percent of Americans characterized race as either "very important" or "extremely important."[2] There is no reason to believe that college students would poll any differently than the nation as a whole. Certainly, professors who introduce discussions of race in their classrooms will attest to the intensity of the feelings that are frequently expressed.

By and large, today's white students do not tolerate overt racism or racial epithets. But they do not understand the fear of racism among African-Americans. They do not understand what one of them called the "gratuitous hostility" of young African-Americans, and a large majority disagree with affirmative action programs. Student debates over race can become very energized. The feelings they voice are so strong that when they debate racial issues many of their professors notice that the students will rarely even look at each other. In college classrooms today, race continues to be what Gunnar Myrdal called an "American dilemma."

Some demographics are in order. About 13 percent of the U.S. population is African-American. About 11 percent of college undergraduates nationwide are African-American. So, for the most part, in talking about the values of today's college students we are talking about mostly white students. In summarizing the views expressed by these students, we can identify three separate trains of thought. The first is a "structuralist" view, which is generally sympathetic to the plight of African-Americans. Factory jobs that paid $17 per hour to the parents of today's blacks have left American cities and workers who would fill those jobs today stand idle on street corners. Global economic transitions do not make room for those left behind. This opinion is voiced by a relatively small group of students. The second is a "culturalist" view that considers the social problems of blacks to be, for the most part, their own fault. Students holding this view also comprise a relatively small group.

The third group usually takes a more complacent view and attracts the majority of students. In their view, there once was racism and discrimination in America but the civil rights movement of the sixties was successful, and we now all have equal opportunity. This "complacent" group generally has had contact with blacks who belong to the middle class. As a group they also believe that black people do not seem to understand how victorious the civil rights movement was and the question they ask most often is this: "Why are blacks so angry?"

BLACK RAGE

The most significant aspect of the views on race held by today's white college students is their ignorance of recent American history. For the most part, these students are not aware of how recently blatant racism was widely accepted by white America. They know that their parents and grandparents love Bill Cosby; they are more familiar with the golfing ability of Tiger Woods than that of Jack Nicklaus; and many would argue that Michael Jordan was a greater athlete than Babe Ruth, probably the greatest athlete ever. They don't know how things used to be. If they are ever going to understand black anger, then American history should not be so quickly forgotten. One attention-getting example helps to make this point.

In 1965, a Gallup Poll asked Americans what they thought about laws that made it a crime for a black person to marry a white person.

Called "miscegenation statutes," these laws would be declared unconstitutional by the U.S. Supreme Court in *Loving v. Virginia* four years
after this poll was taken. When students today are polled for their opinion about miscegenation statutes, there will occasionally be a student
who is familiar with the history of miscegenation statutes and the
Loving case. But for the most part they have never heard of the fact that
in the America of their parents' youth, racial intermarriage was a felony,
punishable in many states by imprisonment. They know that America is
the land of "equal justice under law" and many of them have friends
who are black. They consider their parents, for the most part,
fair-minded people and assume that if the Court struck down such laws,
it must have happened sometime in the 19th century. They also estimate
that the response to the 1965 Gallup Poll question about miscegenation probably resulted in no more than a small handful of pathological
racists who would favor such a law. "Surely not more than 10 percent,"
is the usual guess. Certainly, neither their parents' generation nor their
grandparents' generation would tolerate such nonsense!

The actual poll results in 1965 indicated that 6 percent had no opinion about miscegenation laws and 46 percent opposed such laws. However, a plurality of 48 percent were in favor of such laws—as recently as
1965! Today's college students find it difficult to believe that their parents' generation would display such unabashedly racist views. Most of
the respondents to that poll who had an opinion believed that government should punish any individual who married another person who
happened to be of a different race. It is difficult for today's college students to comprehend the level of racism that existed so recently in
American history.

Polling students today on the issue of miscegenation statutes usually
results in unanimous opposition to them, and students are frequently
shocked that such laws ever existed at all. It is likely that at least a few of
the "culturalist" students are secretly in favor of these statutes but are
reluctant to expose their opinion to the rest of the class. Nevertheless,
there is nothing remotely close to the 48 percent that supported those
statutes in the 1965 Gallup Poll. Times truly have changed and, along
with the times, the nature of the race discussion has changed.

To frame the question in its broadest terms, we need to ask: "Should
the government do more or should the government do less in the effort
to improve the life of African-Americans?" Are blacks given fair treatment today? Are blacks give preferential treatment today? Are affirma-
tive-action programs a form of "reverse discrimination?" Most

important, why are relations between the races still as strained as they are?

Often during these class discussions, professors will notice that white and black students have a very different understanding of both African-American history and the present conditions of the ghettoes of American cities. For instance, white students frequently relate incidents in which black contemporaries of theirs have demonstrated behavior that seemed to them to be "gratuitously hostile," as one white student put it, or at the very least unusually rude. These students genuinely wonder why blacks seem so angry.

It should be pointed out that these are not students who would be considered "racist" by their parents' generation. Generally, these are white students who have expressed a belief in the importance of equal treatment for blacks, who have been shocked by the Gallup Poll about miscegenation and who have stated their moral repugnance for racism. Why, they ask, do so many blacks seem hostile to whites? For example, why is it that the use of the "N word" is so infuriating to blacks when they regularly use it among themselves in a seemingly lighthearted manner? Is this not a double standard? Is this not hypocritical? Why do so many of their African-American contemporaries demonstrate that "gratuitous hostility" toward whites?

One Irish professor referenced his own cultural heritage to answer this question. As an Irishman whose ancestors were brutalized for centuries by English landlords, his answer came from the heart. Part of Irish history includes the ugly fact that some English landlords demanded the sexual services of the wives of their Irish tenant farmers and in many cases these unions resulted in offspring who were half English. If an Englishman referred to these encounters and suggested that it may have resulted in an improved gene pool among this Irish professor's ancestors, he believed that his reaction might well be considered "gratuitously hostile," which was probably a gross understatement.

If, for that matter, an Irish acquaintance called him a "mick" or a "donkey," it would certainly be less offensive than if the term were used by an Englishman. So, the "N word," with its even heavier baggage of hate and domination, has to be understood in the social and historical circumstances in which it is used. And so must the attitude of young African-Americans who can still remember their mothers and grandmothers treated dismissively—if not actually brutalized—by the majority of white society. Many white Americans in those days routinely used the "N word" to refer to all African-Americans, including the family elders of today's black college students. That 48 percent of respondents who told the Gallup pollsters that it should be a felony for a white person and a black person to get married did not exist in a vacuum.

While their parents may have had to live in a society that forced them to passively accept racial epithets from whites, today's black students do not. Nonetheless, for some African-Americans, the memory of the humiliation endured by earlier generations is an ongoing source of anger.

THE DEBATE: CULTURALISTS VERSUS STRUCTURALISTS

The "culturalist" perspective holds that all behavior is rooted in character. Culturalists argue that blacks do not have the same ambition, self-discipline, and moral standards that are required to succeed in the American free-market economy. These students inevitably point to an out-of-wedlock birth rate of 60 percent among African-Americans and a homicide rate that accounts for over half of all the homicides in the nation.

This argument suggests that the high levels of poverty among blacks is attributable to the high rate of single-parent families and that the homicide rate grows out of a "cultural" tolerance for violence in general in the black community. In other words, problems besetting today's African-Americans are a result of "black culture" and no government programs or intervention can address the causes of those problems.

This view is taken by a small but vocal group of students and it is almost always filled with anecdotal evidence that supports its conclusions. Examples of "welfare mothers" getting pregnant and selling food stamps for alcohol while their boyfriends sell drugs in order to buy yet another gold chain are presented again and again as evidence of moral failure.

The initial response of the "structuralist" students is rarely persuasive. Members of this group—generally a coalition of blacks, liberal whites and Hispanics—make generalized references to deplorable conditions in urban ghettoes, inequality in educational and economic opportunity, and racism in the criminal justice system. But, for the most part, they are unable to produce any hard and fast data to support their intuitive views. At this point in the discussion, it is a good educational move to set up a formal debate on these issues.

It is usually wise to restrict these debates to specific questions rather than allow a free-form, rambling discussion to take place. Students from each perspective can be asked to do the research and prepare their arguments about the problems of African-Americans concerning a handful of issues. These might include areas like violence, drugs, education, jobs, and marriage. What are the facts about the rate at which blacks are involved in violence and drugs and what success or failure have they achieved in the areas of education, jobs, and marriage? Finally, what are the underlying causes of this situation? The resulting debate is always very lively and very often the same points are made by the opposing sides.

BLACK VIOLENCE

The homicide rate in the United States is astronomical. No other industrial democracy has anything close to our problem with homicide. Moreover, as the culturalists love to point out, even though blacks constitute just 12 percent of the population, they are responsible for around half of all homicides. These facts remain undisputed by the structuralist debaters and, frankly, this part of the debate is pretty much conceded to the culturalists. However, there are sometimes a few worthwhile rejoinders made by the structuralists.

The homicide rate among the poor is always higher than it is among the middle class. This is true everywhere and the poverty that is so widespread among African-Americans is certainly a factor in explaining their higher rates of homicide. In fact, one student comparing homicide rates of poor whites in Appalachia with that of upper-middle-class, educated blacks found the white rate actually higher.

Furthermore, the rates of homicide are much higher in the American South. White Southerners have a homicide rate that is exponentially higher than their counterparts in the North. No one is quite sure why violence is so much more prevalent in the South but the disparity in homicide rates between the North and the South is startling. Until the last few generations, almost all African-Americans lived in the South and shared in a very violent Southern culture. Homicide rates for African-Americans whose ancestors have lived in the North for many generations are lower than for those who have migrated from the South more recently.

Moreover, the disparity between black and white homicide rates diminishes significantly if we compare the homicide rate of Southern whites to the homicide rate of blacks born and raised in the North. In addition, the homicide rates among blacks from the West Indies is substantially lower than that of African-Americans. Nonetheless, the structuralist students wind up conceding that the homicide rate among African-Americans is significantly higher than that of whites. This first round goes to the culturalists.

DRUGS AND RACE

The culturalists believe that blacks are far more likely to get involved with drugs than are whites. They point to the fact that 74 percent of people incarcerated for drug offenses are African-Americans and claim that this statistic supports their argument.While the structuralists concede that blacks are disproportionately involved in homicide, they do not concede the argument when it comes to drugs. They produce current research about drug use in the United States that is very surprising to the other side. Blacks are slightly less likely than whites to use alcohol, far less likely than whites to use tobacco, and only slightly more likely than whites to use other drugs.

According to the Sentencing Commission (a Washington, D.C.-based think tank), blacks make up about 12.5 percent of the population and just 13 percent of all drug users. However, they constitute 35 percent of all drug arrests, 55 percent of all drug-related convictions, and (yes, the culturalists are correct) 74 percent of all prison admissions for drug offenses. Why did this happen? If blacks are just 13 percent of the drug users, why do they make up 74 percent of those admitted to prison for drug offenses?

The answer lies in the differing methods of marketing drugs. Whites tend to sell drugs in their homes or their dormitories or their office suites. Blacks sell drugs openly on the street. When political leaders pressure the police to come up with big numbers in drug busts, the easiest target is the street corner in the black neighborhoods. The higher number of black arrests increases the likelihood of a prison sentence. Hence, the disproportionate numbers of black drug offenders sentenced to prison each year for the past two decades. This outcome was preordained when it was decided to "get tough" on drugs.

In other words, when the Reagan administration first announced a zero tolerance policy for drug sales, police everywhere were put under pressure to run up the numbers of drug arrests. Police, who would inevitably find it difficult to arrest white drug dealers selling in their homes, offices, and dormitories, would turn to street dealers in frustration. And everyone already knew the color of those street dealers. Blacks are not disproportionately involved in drug use but the criminal justice system certainly makes it appear otherwise.

Generally, the structuralists win this round of the debate.

BLACK EDUCATION

In the sixty years that the Gallup organization has asked the public their *Most Important Problem* question, the highest response that *education* ever received came in March 2000, when respondents cited education as the number-one problem facing the nation. Education beat out taxes, crime, family breakdown, and health care.

It may well be that the most important function of any political system is to provide citizens with an opportunity for an adequate education. Certainly, in the United States, more tax dollars are spent on education than on any other single governmental function. How that money should be spent is a subject of perennial debate among the different political parties and today that debate seems to be more intense than ever before.

The culturalists delight in presenting SAT scores that show higher scores among whites than blacks. This, they argue, demonstrates that blacks cannot ever do as well in school as whites because they have genetically determined intellectual deficiencies. In recent years, many professors have expressed surprise at how many of their students are familiar with *The Bell Curve,* a bestseller by Charles Murray and Richard Hernstein. In that controversial book, the authors flirt with the view that educational inequality is rooted in biological inequality. While this may not have been their intent, culturalist students have seized upon this study and argue that it confirms their own views.

A second school of thought among the culturalists is less extreme. They argue that even if there are no genetic differences between black and white students, there are cultural differences, which result in blacks being less interested in academic achievement. Why, they ask, if blacks are genuinely interested in education, aren't those public libraries at the edge of housing projects overflowing with visitors every afternoon? Why are there so few computers in middle-class black homes? Both of these groups conclude that investing more tax dollars in ghetto schools amounts to throwing good money after bad. If African-Americans are less able to achieve academically or less interested in academic achievement, then why waste money bringing their schools up to the same level as white schools in wealthy suburban areas?

The structuralists respond with some interesting data. One student asked how the SATs could be a reflection of "genetically determined intellect" when his roommate, for a hefty sum of money, had taken the Princeton Review for the SATs and improved his score by over 200 points. Did the review course alter his roommate's genes? Are these tests not influenced by the quality of your early education? If the black scores are truly a result of their "genes" then why have the black scores improved over the past quarter-century? Are their genes changing?

And what about educational achievement? Before the Civil Rights Act of 1964 banned discrimination in educational opportunity, the rate at which blacks graduated from high school was around half of the white rate. Today, there is virtually no difference in the rate of high school graduation. More genetic changes?

However, are African-American schools offering the kind of education that will lead to good jobs? Every Chamber of Commerce in the nation is currently trying to find a work force that has been educated in the kind of high-tech, cognitive skills needed by the new economy. Throughout the American business community—and especially in the Sunbelt—there is a critical shortage of workers skilled in information technology. Since it is not possible to attract industry without an educated labor force, school districts everywhere are trying to educate their students in the skills necessary to accommodate the needs of 21st century, global corporations.

In today's global economy, graduates of American schools look at a future in which they must compete for jobs with their counterparts throughout the industrialized world, including the Asian trading bloc led by Japan, and the European Union led by Germany. Employers look for job applicants with well-developed skills in literacy, numeracy, and the cognitive technologies. How American graduates fare in this competition will be largely a result of what kind of schools we offer them, but it is clearly within our ability to see to it that our graduates can compete successfully with Hans from Berlin and Yoshiro from Tokyo.

Unfortunately, the quality of education that is offered to American children varies widely. There are enormous differences in the funding black and white American students receive in their first twelve years of schooling. To a very large extent, the amount of tax dollars spent on the education of a child in the United States today depends on what her zip code is. Consider the case of Sandy and Leon:

If Money Doesn't Matter, Why Do They Spend so Much on White Schools?

Sandy is a freshman in Great Neck High School on Long Island. Leon is a freshman in Theodore Roosevelt High in the South Bronx. Both hope to do well in high school, go to a good college, and perhaps go to graduate school. In Great Neck, the average public school student has about $17,000 per year spent on his education. It is a first-rate education, and the graduates of the Great Neck schools traditionally do very well competing in the global labor market. About ten miles away from Great Neck—as the crow flies—the public schools of the South Bronx attempt to offer their students an education that will help them compete just as well in the labor market as the Great Neck graduates. Each student in the South Bronx, however, has only around $6,000 per year spent on her education. The graduates of the South Bronx schools traditionally do not do well competing on the global labor market.

Structuralist students jump on this example. How can ghetto students ever hope to pull themselves up when they are condemned to inferior schools with inadequate funding? The more studious of the culturalists will sometimes cite the Coleman Report—or one of its progeny—to support the idea that more funding would not substantially improve educational outcomes. Coleman argued that schools, by themselves, cannot cure poverty and that poverty causes poor educational achievement. So the debate usually comes down to this: Can the government improve the academic performance of blacks by increasing the funding of their schools?

The culturalists argue the "No" position. They point to the $8 billion that the federal government already spends on Title 1 remedial education and ask what good it has all done. They point to various studies that support their conclusions. Generally, these are respected studies that conclude that the academic underachievement of black middle-class students is attributable to differences between black and white child-rearing habits and peer culture.

Black parents, these studies conclude, are not inclined to read to their children, take them on trips, on explain the reason for rules; instead, they rule by edict. The culturalist students ask what government can do about such cultural attitudes? The structuralists respond with their own research. They cite a Michael Katz examination of the famous Gatreaux experiment in Chicago, in which families were given subsidies to move to the suburbs from high-poverty neighborhoods. Once these families had relocated, their children experienced far more academic success than they had in ghetto schools.[3] A second study which students have found impressive is Success for All. Begun by Robert Slavin and his colleagues at Johns Hopkins University in the late 1980s, Success for All (SFA) is a reform program serving children placed at risk for school failure. Its early intervention efforts with poor black students have shown strong evidence of positive effects on student achievement.[4]

In the minds of the students who judge the debate, the research tends to result in a draw. It would appear that there are some programs that actually can improve the performance of black students but these programs are very expensive. Should we spend such large sums on these programs? It would appear that the answer to that question depends on whose ox is being gored. Students whose families would benefit from such programs tend to favor them. Students whose families are in high tax brackets—and would have to pay for those programs—tend to reject them.

It is appropriate to end this segment of the debate with an observation made by Christopher Jencks, the distinguished Harvard professor. According to Jencks, the seminal problem facing the American political system is this: How do we get white, suburban voters to tax themselves enough to fund the public schools of the inner cities in such a way that the inner-city graduates will be able to successfully compete for jobs with other graduates—including the children of those same white, suburban voters?

BLACKS AND THE JOB MARKET

Why is it that one out of ten whites and one out of four blacks are living under the poverty level? Why is the median per capita income of blacks about 60 percent that of whites? The culturalists again blame character and argue that blacks do not want to work. The structuralists respond with a collection of research studies that demonstrates the eagerness for work among black youth. For instance, one study showed that for every fast-food job opening in Harlem, there were fourteen applicants. Another emphasized the thousands of young black recruits who were rejected by the military every year, clearly a difficult and low-paying job. How can the culturalists say that these people do not want to work?

A third study frequently cited by structuralist students shows that labor force participation among blacks used to be higher than for whites. The study demonstrated that labor force participation of white males declined between 1940 and 1980 from 82 percent to 76 percent; while for blacks the numbers fell from 84 percent to 67 percent. In other words, before recent changes in the job market, blacks were slightly more likely to be employed than whites. More interesting is the question of what happened to black participation in the labor market in recent years. The structuralists produce research studies that provide a pretty good answer.

In the fifties and sixties, massive black migration from the South to North filled the need for industrial workers in the factories of the post-war economic boom. In the seventies and eighties the rapid "deindustrialization" of the American economy began and it quickly changed the industrial base of the economy to a service base where blacks—especially black males—did not fare well. This industrial transition resulted in decreases in blue-collar, clerical, and sales jobs in Northern metropolises. In short, the bottom fell out in urban industrial demand for the poorly educated. Where do black males fit in a service-based economy that no longer needs strong backs but has an overwhelming need for graduates of excellent schools?

Another part of this problem is the "spatial-mismatch" dilemma. At the same time that urban areas were losing their factories, the suburban rings of every Northern metropolis saw increases in all classifications of jobs. Unfortunately, ghetto workers anxious to take these jobs often had no practical way of getting to them. Public transportation systems do not provide effective methods for inner-city urban workers to get to low-wage suburban jobs. So, the structuralists ask, how much of the black unemployment and underemployment problem is "cultural" and how much is "structural"?

BLACKS AND MARRIAGE

Culturalists stress the fact that the out-of-wedlock birth rate among blacks is double that of whites. They also argue that when we compare two-parent black households with their white counterparts, the gap between income decreases substantially. Why don't these people get married and support their children the way whites do? Part of the reason, according to the structuralists, is the lack of "marriageable males" in the black community.

Studies of this phenomenon done by William Julius Wilson found that the African-American "male marriageable pool index" reveals a long-term decline in the proportion of black men who are in a position to support a family. Citing Wilson, the structuralists argue that this has been caused by the movement of industry from North to South and West and, more so, from central cities to suburbs. This is the same point that they have made in their discussion of blacks and jobs. But it has also been exacerbated by enormous numbers of young black males being sent to jail or prison (over one-third of all black men in their twenties are under the control of the criminal justice system).

All told, Wilson found that there were only 56 employed black men for every 100 black women in the Northeast between the ages of twenty and forty-four. Significant numbers are locked up or dead; but more are simply unemployed. His point is this: There is some kind of minimum threshold for earnings that must be reached before a man can be considered a serious candidate for marriage. With the growing globalization of the new economy, more and more black males do not reach that threshold. The structuralist students frequently suggest that doubling the minimum wage would push so many low-income couples over that elusive threshold that the out-of-wedlock birth rate would fall dramatically.

AN INVESTMENT IN PEOPLE

Many political commentators today look back on Lyndon Johnson's war on poverty, launched as part of the Great Society initiatives, and denounce it as a tragic waste of government dollars. It is a program that is almost universally condemned as being filled with waste, fraud, and abuse. Except when you talk about it to someone who was actually there.

There is no question that enormous mistakes were made. You only have to read Daniel Patrick Moynihan's book *Maximum Feasible Misunderstanding* to get an idea of how badly the program was handled by bureaucrats. But at the street level, many remember success stories that live in their hearts rather than in the revisionist accounts of today's commentators. One such account comes from the same person who worked with Anthony and Victor Davis.

A few years after finishing college, he was working as a detached street club worker on the lower east side of Manhattan. One Friday afternoon his supervisor came down to the street corner where he worked. He carried with him seventeen inch-thick forms from the federal government. They were written in very small print and he dreaded the prospect of having to read them. This was the beginning of affirmative action programs, and he could not believe what he was reading.

Up until that point, there was no possibility that any of the teenagers with whom he worked would ever get a college degree. Colleges were expensive and these students came from welfare or low-wage families. The City University of New York was free but it was known as "the poor man's Harvard" because of the stringent academic requirements for admission. When anyone had ever asked him about the possibility of education beyond high school—or, more often, instead of high school—his answer was to recommend a cosmetology school for the females and a truck driving school for the males. College was just out of the question.

Now he found himself reading through these forms labeled EOPS (Educational Opportunity Programs). Could it be that he was reading it correctly? A full scholarship to the State University of New York (SUNY) for any "minority group student" who graduated from high school? They did not need straight As or scores of 1400 or better on the SATs. Just a high school diploma.

He started seeking out those few teenagers who had actually remained in school until their senior year. (The dropout rate at these high schools was over 80 percent.) These young people were very skeptical about what he was suggesting, but still too curious to just ignore him. The whole concept was just too good to be true. The federal government was ostensibly offering them a full scholarship—tuition, room, board, books, even a $15 per week allowance—at a major university. It was as if they had won the lottery.

Within a week or two, he had identified thirteen students who were still in school, had reached their senior year, and had a good chance of actually graduating. All of them were interested in this new proposal—very interested. He spoke with their parents. He helped them fill out their applications and he helped them compose their essay on why they wanted to go to college. He offered to go with them to Albany to see the campus and they drove the 150 miles in three borrowed cars. They may as well have been going to Mars.

These were ghetto teenagers who saw a good deal of violence on their streets and lived with a high level of danger on a daily basis. Nonetheless, walking across the rolling hills of the SUNY–Albany campus, they were more fearful than he had ever seen them. He could feel their discomfort. Their clothes, they said, suddenly felt too loud; walking the walk and talking the talk suddenly seemed out of place; the color of their skin suddenly stood out among the middle-class white students who milled about them. Still, they stuck it out. They spent the weekend and returned home confident that they were heading for college in the fall.

Eventually, eleven of them graduated from college. It took them all more than four years and one of them was killed by her husband a year after her graduation. But many of them stayed in touch over the years and there were some outstanding successes in that group. Among the graduates there were a couple of teachers, a few business executives, even one who was voted "Man of the Year" in his state. Today their stories are very different from the expectations one would have had for them before this EOPS program started.

Richie was one of six boys raised by a welfare mother on the lower east side. His older brother was killed in a drug deal when Richie was just starting high school. His younger brother spent most of his life in prison because of his heroin habit. Today Richie is a Ph.D. and the vice president of a college.

Shirley was one of the thirteen. Today she has a master's degree and works as a minority recruiter at an Ivy League college. Shirley had an older sister, Serena, who was every bit as smart and hard working as a teenager. But Serena was two years older than Shirley and when she graduated from high school there was no EOPS. Serena still lives in the same building in which she and Shirley grew up and has spent most of her adult life on and off welfare. Shirley says she feels guilty that she is afraid to bring her kids down to the old neighborhood to visit their cousins and their Aunt Serena. She feels the late-model BMW she drives would not be safe parked on the street.

Finally, there was Chile. Chile was a guy who sold heroin at Seward Park High School. Narcotics officers tried to get him many times but he was very careful about his operation. The street club worker always regretted never being able to prove what everyone knew Chile was doing. Long after he left the job, he ran into a colleague he had worked with there. They spent a couple of hours reminiscing about the old days. They ran names past each other to see with whom they were still in touch or what they had heard about the old gang. "Remember Chile?" the friend asked. "What do you think Chile is doing now?" The other assumed that the correct answer to the question was something like fifteen years to life in Attica but he confessed that he had no idea.

"He's a doctor," his friend said.

"We must be talking about a different guy," the other argued. "Chile was a drug addict; he was bad news. We could never get him."

"He never used it. He only sold it. I got him into college and later he got into medical school. He practices in the old neighborhood."

In the mind of the former street club worker, Chile was probably still a drug dealer but now he got to use a prescription pad. Still, there seemed to be a message here. Whatever the average medical doctor pays in federal income taxes over the course of his career has to be a lot more than the cost of those EOPS scholarships. The annual cost back in those days was about $4,000. Dr. Chile has to have paid back that investment many times over—and that does not include the annual cost of keeping him in the prison cell he would probably be occupying today if they had never brought those EOPS forms down to the lower east side street corner. Government investment in people can bring a payoff that is difficult to predict.

NOTES

1. G. Myrdal, *An American Dilemma* (Harper & Bros., 1944).
2. G. Gallup, *The Gallup Poll Monthly* (Princeton, NJ: The Gallup Poll, January, 2000).
3. J. Traub, "What no school can do," *New York Times Magazine*, 16 January 2000, 52–57, 68, 81, 90–91.
4. R.E. Slavin, N.A. Madden, L.J. Dolan, B.A. Wasik, S.M. Ross, L.J. Smith, & M. Dianda, "Success for all: A summary of the research," *Journal of Education for Students Placed at Risk* 1 (1): 41–76 (1996).

SUGGESTED READINGS

Anderson, J. (1988). Cognitive styles and mutlicultural populations. *Journal of Teacher Education*, 39(1), 2–9.

Branch, T. (1988). *Parting the waters: America in the King years, 1954–63.* New York: Simon and Schuster.

Jencks, C. (1991). Urban underclass and the poverty paradox. In *The Urban Underclass* (p. 171). Washington, DC: The Brookings Institute .

Robinson, R. (2000). *The debt: What America owes to blacks.* New York: Dutton.

Rosenfeld, M. (1993). *Affirmative action and justice: A philosophical and constitutional inquiry.* New Haven, CT: Yale University Press.

Wright, B. (1996). *Black justice in a white world: A memoir.* New York: Barricade Books.

Chapter 9

Drugs

If more prisons are the answer, how well do we understand the question?
"In dealing with drugs we are forced to choose between a crime problem and a public health problem. . . . It may be that drug addiction is one of the problems that government simply cannot solve."
Senator Daniel Patrick Moynihan, 1996

The majority of college students today have smoked marijuana at some point in their lives. A large percentage of them continue to do so, either on a regular or an intermittent basis. They generally do not consider pot an important part of the debate over the drug problem. National polls on marijuana use for the last thirty years of the 20th century showed an uninterrupted climb in the number of respondents who had tried marijuana. From just 4 percent in 1969, it reached 34 percent in 1999[1] and that is for the nation as a whole. Among college students, the numbers are unquestionably higher. Furthermore, legalization of marijuana is an idea that has also garnered greater support among the young. A recent Gallup poll indicated that while 34 percent of the nation as a whole supported legalization, among those under thirty years of age the support reached 44 percent.

When today's college students discuss the drug problem, they refer to cocaine, heroin, amphetamines, hallucinogens, Ecstasy, and Rophynol. In addition, more and more students insist on including alcohol in any discussion of the drug problem. This may be because of the increasing number of families that have experienced serious problems with alcohol. For instance, a Gallup poll in 1999 asked if alcohol had presented a problem for the respondent's family. The public at large gave the highest positive response since the question was first asked in 1947, namely 36 percent. However, respondents in the eighteen- to twenty-nine-year-old age group gave a 42 percent positive response, the highest positive response of any age group.

This generation seems better informed about drugs than any earlier generation and they have some pretty strong opinions about it. These students are generally aware that responsible estimates suggest that as many as 90 million Americans have used illegal drugs. They also know that media attention to the drug problem has waned in recent years. One study pointed out that TV networks used to run over 400 drug stories a year and that they now air only about 40 a year. In other words, they are aware that Americans are starting to think of the drug problem as a symptom of more fundamental social and spiritual problems, rather than the problem itself. They are very skeptical about government policies concerning drugs.

In college classes today, the debate over drugs often comes down to two extremes: the "drug warriors" and the "free marketeers." In a curious mix of the political left and the political right, the debate over what the government should do about the problem is indeed unique. The line between liberal and conservative seems to blur and students who rarely agree with each other on most issues wind up as "strange bedfellows."

A second unique aspect to this debate is the fact that, unlike so many other discussions, this debate often has a clear-cut winner. One student quoted Senator Daniel Patrick Moynihan's statement about drugs in a recent book. "It may be," wrote the senator, "that drug addiction is one of the problems government cannot solve."[2] This position resonates with today's students.

In the debates about appropriate drug policy, the drug warrior position seems to crumble and something of a consensus is achieved around the "free marketeer" position. The "drug warriors" argue that we have a moral obligation to continue the war on the supply of drugs and that we may be getting closer to controlling the drug problem. They point to falling rates of drug use and to the 400,000 inmates nationwide who are serving time for drug offenses and argue that we need to redouble our efforts. Very often this position is taken by students who have previously expressed liberal views about welfare, food stamps, low-income housing, and other programs in which government has helped solve social problems. But they are joined by students who have previously expressed conservative views about the benefits of prison expansion and a "get tough" approach to crime.

The "free marketeers," on the other hand, say drugs constitute a spiritual or psychological problem that law enforcement will never resolve. Moreover, they claim that it is immoral to imprison an individual who is not hurting anyone but himself. They urge a war on the *demand* for drugs rather than on the *supply* of drugs, similar to the war on the demand for tobacco. They repeatedly cite the law of "supply and demand" and argue that the supply of drugs will never be reduced so long as there are profits to be made. Again students express very strong opinions on this topic.

One of these free marketeers was a parole officer for the state of New York. He had a caseload made up of numerous heroin addicts and would regularly take urine from a parolee, send it to a lab, and send parolees found to be "dirty" back to prison. There was no court hearing; there was no appeal of his judgment; the parolee simply went back to a state prison and stayed there for a minimum of nine months. One of the parolees, whom he considered one of the "success stories," was a man named Ellsworth. His story is worth telling here:

The Oblivion Seeker

Ellsworth began using drugs when he was in his early teens. He liked them a lot. By age sixteen he was using heroin; by eighteen he was addicted. He began to steal in order to support his habit and he wound up serving several short jail terms before finally being sent to prison for three armed robberies of gas stations on Long Island. He served two years and was given drug rehabilitation therapy during that time. He was twenty-seven years old when he was paroled from prison and sent home. Despite many previous relapses into heroin use, he was determined to remain heroin free for the rest of his life and, to the best of our knowledge, he succeeded in that regard. This made Ellsworth one of the few addicts who managed to quit heroin while still in his twenties. Unfortunately, Ellsworth drank something between one and two quarts of vodka every day and remained almost as incapacitated from alcohol as he had been from heroin.

Does Ellsworth's story suggest that drugs are more of a spiritual problem than one for law enforcement? Could it be that drugs are not an external problem, where chemicals seduce unwilling victims but rather a problem of people seeking oblivion? Does it matter whether Ellsworth finds that oblivion in vodka rather than in heroin? Drug warrior students ordinarily respond to this question by pointing out that vodka is much less expensive than heroin so that Ellsworth would have to commit fewer crimes to secure an adequate supply of alcohol, possibly no crime at all. However, other students point out that this is circular reasoning. They argue that vodka is cheap because there are no laws banning it. It is, they say, the laws prohibiting drugs that raise the price and guarantee large drug profits.

For example, a newspaper article that one student brought to class stated that in June 1996 a pack of Marlboros sold for $3 in the San Francisco jail. On July 1, cigarettes were banned in the jail. By August 1, that pack of Marlboros was selling on the jail's black market for $120. Prohibition meant profits. Will the increased cost mean that there are fewer buyers? Or will a falling price invite a greater number of consumers? Are there a fixed number of drug users who will pay any price for their drugs or are there many others who have been scared away from drugs because of the high price? The conjectures are widespread and deeply felt.

THE FREE MARKETEER ARGUMENT

The "drug warrior" argument is that government should mobilize all its resources for an all-out war on the supply of drugs in this country. If we "get tough" enough, we will end the problem. The free marketeers' argument is to ignore the supply and attack the demand, the way we attacked the demand for cigarettes. How, they ask, can we ever even dream of keeping drugs out of a free society if we cannot even keep them away from inmates of maximum-security prisons? They argue that for at least the last thirty years, the U.S. government has been waging one war on drugs after another. Every time a president or a governor announces a new war on drugs, it seems as though a kind of media amnesia sets in about the last war on drugs, as if it never happened. These wars, they point out, always have three parts: interdiction, prevention, and treatment.

The problem is this: Interdiction is aimed at eliminating or reducing the supply, which has never worked. If it had, these student researchers report, then they would have difficulty finding drugs to buy. They do not. In their minds, the law of supply and demand, predetermines that every war on supply is doomed from the beginning. Moreover, and per-haps most disturbing, is the argument that the public in general is aware of this monumental failure.

In a report on the subject, one student presented some Gallup polls concerning the government's effort to control drugs. From 1972 through 1999, Gallup has asked how much progress respondents feel is being made in coping with the problem of illegal drugs. While the numbers have varied somewhat over the years, there has never been a year in which the majority of respondents failed to indicate that no progress was being made.[3] In other words, most Americans believe that in the last three decades the government's costly war on drugs has had absolutely no impact.

It is difficult to defend the "war on supply" or to be hopeful about its future prospects. Thirty years ago the Drug Enforcement Agency—called BNDD (Bureau of Narcotics and Dangerous Drugs) at the time—published an estimate of what percentage of all drugs sold on America's streets were seized by law enforcement. Their estimate at the time was 5 percent. In other words, 95 percent of all drugs got through to the users despite all our efforts to interdict them.

Today our interdiction efforts are far more substantial then they were back then. We have AWAC (Airborne Warning and Control Sys-tem) planes hunting down drug dealers flying their drugs over the bor-der; we have dogs at airports sniffing everyone's luggage; we have random urine testing of employees and locker searches of school chil-dren; we have sheriffs' departments spraying poisonous chemicals on marijuana crops.

How are we doing? Well, the sad truth is that little has changed. Drugs are as readily available as ever on America's streets and even DEA concedes that we are still seizing only about 5 percent of all drugs sold in the country. Is the war on drugs working? Is there any sign that it will ever work to eliminate, or even reduce, the supply of drugs? As Senator Moynihan told a Senate committee on drug abuse, "Other than to raise the price of drugs somewhat, drug interdiction is not going to have the slightest effect on supply."[4]

What about drug treatment efforts? Students today are familiar with the research studies demonstrating that drug treatment programs can be effective. Nonetheless, they see that very little money is spent on drug treatment in today's prisons and, even on the outside, it is difficult to find openings in drug treatment programs. Most government spending on drugs is aimed at interdicting the supply, an effort that has never produced encouraging results.

The free marketeer students view with enormous suspicion—some might call it cynicism—this pattern of investing all our available funds in a war on supply, which is doomed, and very little on treatment or prevention, which could actually reduce demand. Is there a method to this madness? Is there a "silent hand" behind all this? A silent hand that is somehow connected to that $100 billion in annual drug profits?

POLITICAL PROTECTION OF DRUG PROFITS?

Cynicism about political leaders has reached an historic high among today's college students. Scandals that have received extraordinary media coverage may underlie this phenomenon; or maybe the kind of "money politics" that characterizes today's political system make it inevitable. Whatever the cause, college students today have few political heroes and relatively little faith in the integrity of their leaders.

Questions about the financing of political campaigns seem to grow more pointed each time a campaign finance reform bill is voted down or another self-defeating drug policy is announced. Students listen as the Republicans charge that the Chinese gave the Democrats contributions in the 1996 election. They hear the Democrats respond that the Republicans are even worse, taking tobacco money to kill the McCain-Feingold campaign finance reform bill. Students shake their heads in despair.

Of course, no one likes the political action committee (PAC) system that arose after the last attempt at campaign finance reform under the Nixon administration. The PACs have turned the American political system into an unseemly contest between massive advertising campaigns, which generally conclude with the victory of the bigger spender. Despite the unpleasant odor that surrounds political contributions, both business and labor interests need to have "access" to their political leaders in order to lobby them effectively. The interests of business and labor will then be served by legislation that advances American interests around the world. In support of the current system, some would argue that it is more true today than ever before that "What is good for General Motors is good for America." Therefore, a percentage of profits from all business and labor groups is routinely set aside to influence future legislation by making contributions to political campaigns.

However, students today have begun to raise a troubling question about the role of lobbying and the establishment of a national drug policy. Why is it, they ask, that we are comfortable talking about how profits from the automobile industry or the tobacco industry or even the alcohol industry influence future legislation, but no one ever looks at political contributions from the drug industry? They are not talking here about Merck or Bristor-Myers Squibb or Johnson & Johnson. Surely a reasonable portion of profits were set aside by such corporations to go to PACs that would lobby in the interest of legislation favorable to the pharmaceutical industry. But, they ask, what about the illicit drug industry? Don't they buy political protection?

Most responsible estimates of the annual profits from illegal drugs sold in the United States are in the neighborhood of $100 billion—about ten times that of the car industry. Obviously, no one knows how much of that profit—if anything—has been contributed by narco-traffickers to American political campaigns. Just how much of the illegal drug profits, students ask, find their way into political action committees? And what kind of influence does it buy? There is no hard evidence that any drug profits go into political campaigns, but interested students press the issue as they explore the ethical questions involved.

Would it not be inconceivable, they argue, to think that this industry is any less in need of political assistance than other industries? How much "access" was bought by profits from illegal drugs being poured into political campaigns? More important, what kind of legislation would a narco-trafficker request from a president or a member of Congress or a governor or a state legislator to whom he had contributed campaign funds? A few semesters ago a student produced an article from the *New York Times* that dealt with the Jorge Cabrera case:

Buying Access

Jorge Cabrera had his photograph taken with Hillary Rodham Clinton and Al Gore at a Christmas party at the White House in 1996. Three weeks later, Cabrera was arrested and charged with importing 6,000 pounds of cocaine. He pleaded guilty and received a sentence of nineteen years in prison, which he is now serving.

Cabrera earned his invitation to the party when a campaign solicitor for the Democratic National Committee (DNC) received
$20,000 from Cabrera the previous fall. (It turned out that the
money came from an account filled with Cabrera's drug profits.)
When DNC officials were informed of this situation by the press,
they returned the money to Cabrera.

If we assume that Cabrera wanted to discuss with the first lady and
the vice president the current laws dealing with drugs, what kinds of
drug policies would best suit his interests? Would you suspect that he
would ask for the war on drugs to be escalated or abandoned? The drug
warriors responded, "Cabrera would naturally want drug laws to be less
punitive so that his business would not be as dangerous and, if caught,
he would serve less time."

The student who discovered the *Times* story then asked, "Would
Cabrera's drug profits increase or decrease if the United States adopted
the more lenient drug laws of European nations?" If the government
repealed all laws against all drugs, what would happen to the drug profits that people like Jorge Cabrera have been making? Would it not be
the same thing that would happen to the profits from selling cigarettes
in the San Francisco jail if the warden repealed the rule against cigarette
use?

She concluded by suggesting that lobbyists representing illicit drug
profits may have indeed been very effective. If, today, $100 is paid on
American streets for a quantity of heroin that actually costs less than a
dollar to produce, what would a withdrawal from the war on drugs do
to the profits currently being made? Would the price not fall to the
point of minimizing the enormous profits that the Jorge Cabreras of
the world have enjoyed for many decades? What will happen to the cost
of marijuana in California or Arizona now that the laws limiting its use
have been relaxed?

Defending the current system is not easy. The argument can be made
that all illegal products are expensive but that does not mean we should
legalize the sale of things like machine guns or nuclear weapons or human babies. Drugs devastate the lives of users and rational governments
should do what they can to discourage their use. The response of the
student—now backed by all of the "free marketeer" students—was to
suggest that a government that was not influenced by drug profits
would do things designed to cut down on drug use. Government officials would spend money on drug treatment and education because
such programs work.

Instead, they argued, we spend money on a very public but self-defeating war on the *supply* of drugs when a war on the *demand* for drugs might actually reduce drug use. Their point, of course, was that the war on supply is a stalking horse behind which the drug profits continue to surge. This highly visible war appeases the public and offers politicians cover from criticism. They are "doing something" about drugs, while at the same time keeping invisible drug profits—and PAC contributions—intact.

This argument is very appealing to the conspiratorial instincts of college students and it gains strength from the cynicism felt by both the right-wing and left-wing students. The strongest response to this argument is based on the personal integrity of political leaders, people who simply would not accept campaign contributions that came from drug profits. But students can see that even the politicians themselves would have no way of knowing how much their PACs were getting from drug profits. PACS with high-minded names, like "Citizens for a Drug-Free Youth," for example, can easily front for drug profiteers. One might wonder how a politician would be able to detect the true nature of such an organization's business and distinguish it from the honest efforts of others. There is currently no limit to the number of PACs that can be created to funnel money to political parties willing to vote in favor of our present approach to drugs. It would not be difficult for drug profiteers to create as many of these PACs as they wished. Students ask, "What legislator would see a problem in agreeing with such staunch and civic-minded contributors seeking to 'protect our schoolyard from that poison' by retaining the current drug laws?" Are they continuing the failed policies in order to protect these PAC contributions?

Every time this subject is discussed with students, a strong drift of sentiment toward the free marketeer position can be sensed. Since we find this position overly cynical, it behooves us to argue that such conspiratorial speculation is fanciful and that, in the real world, operators like Jorge Cabrera are more likely to wind up behind bars than they are to be setting national drug policy. But it is difficult not to notice the skepticism in the eyes of students.

NOTES

1. G. Gallup, *The Gallup Poll Monthly* (Princeton, NJ: The Gallup Poll, November 3, 1999).

2. D. P. Moynihan, *Miles to go: A personal history of social policy* (Cambridge, MA: Harvard University Press, 1996), 211.

3. G. Gallup, *The Gallup Poll Monthly* (Princeton, NJ: The Gallup Poll, April 9, 1999).

4. D.P. Moynihan, *Miles to go: A personal history of social policy* (Cambridge, MA: Harvard University Press, 1996), 203.

SUGGESTED READINGS

Currie, E. (1993). *Reckoning: Drugs, the cities and the American future*. New York: Hill and Wang.

Nadelman, E.A. (1989, September). Drug prohibition in the United States: Costs, consequences and alternatives. *Science*, 245, 27.

National Institute on Drugs and Alcohol. (1991). *National household survey of drug abuse, population estimates*. Washington, DC: U.S. Government Printing Office.

Trebach, A., & Engelsman, E. (1989, Summer). Why not decriminalize? *NPQ*, 40–45.

Epilogue: Has the Moral Reasoning of College Students Changed?

In 1999 a Gallup poll asked Americans if we had become "too permissive" as a society and whether they were "optimistic" about the future of American morality.[1] Only 23 percent of respondents were optimistic about our moral future; 64 percent felt our society had become "too permissive."

In the quarter-century that we have taught education, law, and politics to college students, however, we have never seen a period when students were more eager than today to discuss fundamental questions about right and wrong. Despite what many others contend, students really are interested in examining their own moral values and reaching some conclusions about what they personally believe is morally correct. We also believe that they value the *logic* inherent in these arguments for the weight of persuasion it is able to carry.

It is almost as if students today sense the rapidity with which the world around them is changing and they need something to hold on to. Globalization of trade, with all its economic ramifications, tells them that the old rules for jobs and careers no longer apply. The information revolution presents constant challenges to them to learn new cognitive technologies with no end in sight. In this milieu, guidelines of any sort are comforting. Moral markers need to be sought out in students' thinking as part of their education and highlighted through the exchange of ideas.

On the whole, education majors tend to be a more optimistic group than are students of law and politics. It may be that as prospective teachers they need to keep hope for the future alive in their hearts. In fact, it is just this hope that seems to draw many to the field. However, a majority of students who take courses in law and politics are considerably more skeptical. As we saw in the early chapters, these students share the widespread public perception that much of the law is superfluous and many lawyers are unethical and avaricious. It is important to disabuse them of the idea that we can all arrive at a "just" solution to our legal/moral dilemmas simply by following our conscience. These students need to consider difficult legal and moral dilemmas and propose just solutions. Regularly they disagree among themselves about what the just thing to do is.

Very often a majority will ultimately come to understand the underlying logic of the existing law. This recognition often leads them to become less dismissive of the legal minds that have created the common law over the last eight centuries and to begin to recognize that the law might *not* be "an ass and an idiot." In other words, they often wind up agreeing with the solution that the law already provides for these dilemmas.

Presenting them with examples of laws that are based on both logic and morality tends to increase their respect for the law. At the same time they understand that there is a need for amending the law on a regular basis when social change brings about a new consensus on moral issues. In its most extreme form, of course, this can drift into decontructionism and the view that right and wrong have nothing to do with the rules. Since everything can be manipulated, the deconstructionists conclude, what appears to be right for one culture at one point may be completely wrong for another culture or at a different time. While this may very well be true, it is important to remember that a nation needs laws to hold itself together. If these modern-day members of the "know nothing party" had their way, they would never again have to study for a final exam. In our classes, that is not always the case.

The urge to change the law in order to more adequately reflect today's moral and political consensus is most often thought of as a "progressive" instinct. Throughout the last few decades, legal changes have generally been led by left-wing forces with the more conservative voices clinging to the status quo. This is no longer completely true. In many colleges, the majority of today's students want to return to less progressive solutions. Issues like school prayer or the death penalty or government regulation present questions that our students often want answered with very traditional solutions.

The general consensus on the campuses of the sixties was left of center and, indeed, on a few issues (e.g., homosexuality or drug policies) the consensus today seems even further to the left. But on many other issues, students' views are far to the right of the sixties consensus. In general, students support the death penalty; they think school prayer should be reinstated; and they believe that government programs should be scaled back. As we see it, the political center on campus today is very different from the political views that our own generation held while in college in "the sixties."

Today that term frequently has those quotation marks around it, even if the seventies and eighties and nineties do not. Everyone old enough to have experienced that turbulent decade (actually extending into the early seventies) understands why mentioning "the sixties" evokes in people such strong memories and intense emotions. Those who were too young to experience it firsthand never quite get it. The students we teach fall into that category.

Explaining the sixties to these students is not easy. Somehow the sum of the parts never adds up to the whole. It was not like anything they have experienced in their lives. It was a time of revolutionary social change, it was a time of almost nonstop protests, and it was a time of some dramatic challenges to the status quo. All over the campuses of the sixties were advocates of utopian social experiments and a collection of radical agitators calling for violent political upheaval. But how do we capture the symbols and the confrontations of that era, the changes in lifestyle, in family relationships and in personal freedoms—areas that continue to be debated more than three decades after the fact?

"The sixties" simply refuse to fade into history. Christian conservatives view the era as some kind of Satanic victory over traditional social values. To the extent that we can read the minds of people on the so-called "American left," we see them still admiring many of the achievements of the era, though they wince at some of its cultural excesses. The challenge to authority raised by that generation (often derisively referred to in our classes as the "flower children") no doubt helped spur on the fight against war, racism, sexism, and environmental pollution. But did it also destroy a sense of personal responsibility? Weaken the family? Produce a scourge of drugs, out-of-wedlock births, and sexually transmitted diseases?

Part of the left—activists for blacks, women, and gays—still argues that the sixties actually changed very little and that America continues to be the same racist, homophobic patriarchy that it was in the fifties. The students we teach have their own views on this.

It is important to understand that the actual time period that made up the sixties is not always clear. The two events that may most accurately symbolize the start and finish of the sixties are the assassination of John F. Kennedy in 1963 and the resignation of Richard Nixon in 1974. Many social scientists explain the etiology of the sixties in terms of demographics and economics. A large segment of the 76 million baby boomers born between 1946 and 1964 came of age in the sixties. The prosperity of the fifties put large amounts of cash in the hands of this demographic bubble and added fuel to the fire.

At the core, the demands of the flower children were essentially for justice. They were asking for a re-evaluation of what the "establishment" considered policies that were just. If we define *justice* as the proper balance between autonomy and social obligation, then how do we strike that balance? True justice, it was felt among our contemporaries in the sixties, required fundamental changes in areas as diverse as the military-industrial complex, race relations, recreational drug use, sexual behavior, poverty programs, freedom of speech, police authority, abortion, and environmental issues. It was a lot more than just long hair and beards.

Today, some of the specifics have changed—students prefer to debate the justice of setting priorities for human organ transplant recipients rather than the injustice of drafting noncollege students for Vietnam—but the underlying question of "What does justice demand?" remains the same.

As we have seen in the preceding three chapters on social justice, students today take a different view of problems like poverty and race and crime and drugs. Generally, they are less enthusiastic than their counterparts in the sixties about the chances of government programs helping the poor. They are more likely to be believers in free market solutions to poverty, and more inclined to blame the poor for their condition.

On matters of race, there are a couple of interesting differences in attitude between these students and those of the sixties. Racial epithets are almost universally viewed as a sure sign of ignorance. Discriminatory laws that were condemned by a small group of radicals in the sixties are today condemned by virtually every student. There appears to be a greater likelihood today for a student to have a friend of a different race, although cafeterias and dormitories still evince an informal segregation. Affirmative action programs, however, are widely condemned by students as a form of reverse discrimination. Two decades ago students were far more inclined to view these programs as both necessary and just. It may be that progress made because of these programs has changed the situation to an extent that, in the minds of today's students, they have outlived their usefulness.

Crime and drugs are problems that today's students have strong opinions about. Like all Americans, students have an exaggerated view of the extent of crime in the United States. They are surprised to see the data that demonstrates our crime rate (with the exception of homicide) is really no different from that of the rest of the industrialized world. They are aware of the dramatic decrease in crime over the past decade and the extraordinary explosion of crime rates in the sixties, but they are shocked to hear that demographers had predicted both phenomena based on the 76 million baby boomers. When this group entered the crime-prone age group in the sixties, the crime rate inevitably boomed; when they outgrew the crime-prone age group in the eighties and nineties, crime rates inevitably fell. Students are surprised at how much their beliefs about crime have been influenced by media distortion.

By and large, students today favor the death penalty in far greater numbers than the students of the sixties did. However, this support has begun to slip in the past few years, perhaps because many DNA tests have shown innocent people languishing on death row.

They also believe prison sentences for violent offenders should be increased. But they are shocked by some of the extremes that various states have gone to in an effort to eliminate crime. Draconian penalties for nonviolent property offenders are something of which they strongly disapprove. This disapproval becomes even more intense when it comes to the punishments handed out for drug offenses. Zero tolerance for drug possession is a policy that an overwhelming majority of students repudiate.

They find one example after another of drug offenders receiving harsher punishment than murderers and rapists. They see more and more tax dollars spent on incarcerating addicts but very little spent on drug treatment or prevention. They know better than their elders that the war on supply has removed just a tiny percentage of drugs from the streets. Students are aware of just how available drugs are and wonder why we continue to fight the futile war on supply. They are very skeptical about the political leaders who continue to assure them that this war can be won.

CONCLUSION

In Victor Hugo's masterpiece, *Les Miserables*, Inspector Javert's single-minded pursuit of Jean Valjean is motivated by his simple belief that "the law is the law is the law." There were no exceptions; there were no shades of gray. There was simply right and wrong. Valjean had broken the law and no matter how unfair the law had been or how exemplary Valjean's life had been for the last quarter-century, he had to be punished.

The moral confusion that exists in the culture of the industrialized world today makes that kind of simplistic absolutism very tempting to large groups of people. Indeed, we can see strong hints of this perspective in the fringe groups of the Christian right and even in popular talk show hosts like Dr. Laura Schlessinger. There is clearly a market for black and white answers concerning moral issues.

The great Enlightenment philosopher, Immanuel Kant, argued in favor of a kind of moral absolutism that demanded adherence to an unambiguous view of right and wrong. Lying, for instance, was wrong, regardless of the circumstances in which the lie was told. So if telling the absolute truth would have devastating effects on another's feelings, perhaps even damage the fragile ego of a child, the morally correct thing to do was to ignore those hurt feelings and tell the truth. There was right and there was wrong, and Kant's "categorical imperative" made the difference between the two objectively clear. From Kant to Javert to Dr. Laura, rules, uncluttered by nuance or modifiers, have always offered a certain reassurance to those confused by moral dilemmas.

Certainly, the challenge to traditional morality by the radicals of the sixties preordained a period of confusion in the aftermath of the "revolution." It should come as no surprise that this moral confusion would be fertile ground for moral absolutists. Surely, the radicalism of an Abby Hoffman as a moral spokesman for his generation would suggest that the reactionary absolutism of a Dr. Laura couldn't be far behind. But caught in the middle of these two extremes, the vast majority of today's college students seems to be accepting of neither.

It may be that we are seeing in this generation a rejection of the radical moral relativism that many of their parents embraced in the sixties and seventies. With the pace of change reaching warp speed in the postindustrial society surrounding these students, it is no wonder that they seek some kind of constancy in moral values. Still, while they seem to want to clarify what they believe is right and wrong, it is rare that students embrace the Kantian absolutism in their moral beliefs.

The Puritanism that undergirded much of American morality in the past does not seem very popular with this generation of students. The sexual pecadillos of political leaders are met with a shrug of the shoulders and a moral outlook that suggests we should "Judge not lest we shall be judged." The majority of these students feel a need for moral standards but are not inclined to accept someone else's party line about what is right and wrong. Instead, they are more likely to look inside themselves to find the certainties that social institutions no longer provide.

On the campus today, students are willing to listen to all the information they can find about moral dilemmas but, ultimately, they will follow the dictates of their own conscience. The Roman jurist Julius Paulus said in the third century, "What is right is not derived from the rule, but the rule arises from our knowledge of what is right." The rules for tomorrow have yet to be written. Let us hope that they are written by people of conscience.

NOTE

1. G. Gallup, *The Gallup Poll Monthly* (Princeton, NJ: The Gallup Poll, February 8, 1999).

SUGGESTED READINGS

Bates, S. (1995, January 8). A textbook of virtues. *New York Times*, Education Life, pp. 4A, 15–18, 44, 46.
Dewey, J. (1909). *Moral principles in education*. Boston: Houghton Mifflin.

Index

About the Authors

JOSEPH DILLON DAVEY is a lawyer, political scientist, and author of numerous articles and books on public policy. Currently he is Associate Professor of Law and Justice at Rowan University of New Jersey.

LINDA DuBOIS DAVEY is Assistant Professor of Education at Hofstra University. She has published numerous articles on education issues.